Magazine Law

Magazine Law is a comprehensive guide to the law for magazine journalists, editors and managers. Written by a barrister experienced in publishing and copyright law and a former magazine journalist and law lecturer, the book addresses the special needs of the magazine industry and explains the laws that regulate what journalists can and cannot publish, and how these laws are applied in everyday situations.

Written specifically for all those in the magazine industry, as well as students of magazine journalism, the book considers issues which directly affect day-to-day practice. The legal and regulatory framework is illustrated with case studies and up-to-date examples of precedent-setting cases.

The authors consider a range of key issues: the legal process and its distinction between criminal and civil law; the role of the courts and reporting court procedure; issues of copyright and passing-off; defamation, fair comment and libel; law for photographers and picture researchers; competitions, lotteries and magazine promotion; sub-editing errors and inaccurate copy; the laws of privacy and trespass; and the many other ethical and professional issues facing journalists.

Codes of Practice published by the Press Complaints Commission and the National Union of Journalists are set out in appendices. A glossary of legal terms is included.

Peter Mason is a barrister specialising in copyright and publishing law.
Derrick Smith is a freelance journalist and media law specialist who has had many years' experience working on newspapers and magazines.

Magazine Law

A Practical Guide

Peter Mason and Derrick Smith

A BLUEPRINT book
published by Routledge
London and New York

First published 1998
by Routledge
11 New Fetter Lane, London EC4P 4EE

Simultaneously published in the USA and Canada
by Routledge
29 West 35th Street, New York, NY 10001

© 1998 Peter Mason & Derrick Smith

Typeset in Times New Roman by Florencetype Ltd, Stoodleigh, Devon
Printed and bound in Great Britain by Redwood Books, Trowbridge,
Wiltshire

British Library Cataloguing in Publication Data
A catalogue record for this book is available from the British Library

Library of Congress Cataloguing in Publication Data
A catalogue record for this book is available from the Library of
Congress

ISBN 0–415–15141–4 (hbk)
     0–415–15142–2 (pbk)

Contents

Figures

Foreword

Every magazine journalist at some time in their career will wish they could remember more of the law talks, seminars or courses they attended. Equally, those who have yet to enter the industry and are studying journalism need a reliable reference source on media law.

The book meets these needs and will be an essential tool in the day-to-day process of writing, subbing, commissioning and publishing magazines. Accuracy and integrity are the mark of professionalism and by knowing what can and cannot be published and appreciating the ethical issues of what appears in print, every journalist can help ensure that their work is of the highest standard.

More than ever before, it is necessary to know, appreciate and adhere to all the agreed codes of practice for our industry. These are clearly set out in this book, adding to its value for any magazine journalist.

Pat Roberts Cairns
Editor-in-Chief, Good Housekeeping
Chair, PTC Editorial Training Committee

Periodicals Training Council

Magazine Law was produced in association with the Periodicals Training Council. The PTC is the magazine industry's training body committed to promoting best practice training and improving the performance of people working in the industry. Its work involves promoting investment in people, assessing and responding to the sector's training and development needs, representing the industry's education and training interests to government, and ensuring the development, review and implementation of standards.

The PTC can be contacted for information on any aspect of the magazine industry's training and development including NVQs, Investors in People, life-long learning, training companies and courses, research, publications and careers advice.

PTC, Queen's House
55/56 Lincoln's Inn Fields
London WC2A 3LJ
Tel: 0171–404 4168
Fax: 0171–404 4167
Email: training@ppa.co.uk

Preface

More than 15,000 full-time and 10,000 freelance journalists are now employed on magazines in Britain and the industry lists about 8,000 titles with an annual turnover in excess of £3.4 billion.

So far no one book has attempted to address the special needs of this army of journalists in those aspects of the law that regulate and seek to delineate what magazines can and cannot publish. The purpose of this book is to provide those journalists with a handy, reader-friendly reference point, training manual and guide. It will help and inform students on magazine journalism and media studies courses; trainees on in-company training programmes; more experienced senior journalists working as writers, sub-editors and production staff on consumer and business-to-business magazines, and house publications in companies, stores, charities, voluntary organisations and other bodies concerned with communicating in print with the public.

Freelance writers and photographers will find in it references that are of particular concern to them, such as assignment of copyright in words and pictures, the use of model release forms, the various contractual relationships with magazine companies and the value of written agreements.

It should be available in press, advertising and public relations departments where a frank and honest understanding between non-publishing executives and periodical journalists, particularly in the sensitive areas of product reviews and performance testing, is essential if magazines are to be free to satisfy the needs of their readers without undue pressure and the fear of litigation either from individuals or manufacturers.

Journalists who wish to be recognised as fully qualified industry practitioners by working towards a National Vocational Qualification (NVQ) in periodical journalism will find that the guide covers much of the ground required to show a knowledge and understanding of media law and ethics.

Because the book is aimed at journalists working on magazines rather than newspapers some aspects of media law discussed in traditional law books have been omitted as having little relevance.

Extra emphasis is provided, however, on the practical problems involved in product performance testing and the differences between libel and malicious falsehoods. This 'need to know' was so clearly demonstrated by inaccurate comment on what has become known as the *Yachting World* case.

In the belief that magazine journalists do not have the time or the inclination to visit law libraries to research cases, citations have been kept to a minimum. The aim is to provide a practical guide to recognising legal principles and to applying them, rather than an ability to recite rules.

Some cases are referred to in more than one chapter. For example, one news story can involve issues of confidence, copyright, contempt of court and defamation. It seemed appropriate to repeat them to support a point of view.

The legal system is outlined in Chapter 1; it deals with the legal process and the distinctions between criminal and civil law and the role of the courts, helping to put the remaining chapters of the book into context.

The most risky and litigation-sensitive area of media law for journalists is defamation and this is dealt with in Chapters 2–6. Particular attention is paid to product testing and reviewing in Chapter 7. The differences between libel and malicious falsehood are explained and the chapter contains a journalist's guide to product testing.

Lawful and unlawful copying of other people's copyright material is discussed in Chapter 8 and particular reference is made to commissioning and the reuse of photographs.

Although contempt of court arises principally out of crime stories, which do not feature heavily in magazines, we do believe all journalists should have some understanding of how and when it can arise, and this is outlined in Chapter 9.

The issues of confidential information and infringement of privacy are closely linked in the minds of many journalists, and although we have tried to dispel this idea to some extent they are dealt with consecutively in Chapters 10 and 11. Appropriately, we have followed this with a look at the question of morals and journalists' approaches to ethical and professional issues, such as conflicts of interests, accepting hospitality and going 'undercover', in Chapter 12.

Many readers' complaints arise out of sub-editing errors; some common pitfalls, such as sloppy punctuation, inaccurate headlines and careless but harmful juxtapositions, are mentioned in Chapter 13.

When a reader does complain it is vital that the correct action is taken promptly and safely, and guidelines on how to handle complaints are set out in Chapter 14.

Often law books do not provide answers to everyday questions such as 'What should I do when someone demands to see my copy before it is published?' So Chapter 15 is a compilation of such questions with suggested replies.

Finally, Chapter 16 examines the impact on editorial training of the intro-duction of NVQs in periodical journalism and their method of assessment is discussed together with some ideas for making media law training more practical.

Chapters end with a checklist for action before and after publication, where appropriate.

If we are thought to have been cautious in some respects it is because we recognise the line to be drawn in publishing between what is legally permissible and what will put you at risk. Decisions in the second category can be made only on a story-by-story basis by editors who know their readers, are in possession of all the evidence and have taken professional legal advice.

In some instances we have omitted names of publications and journalists either to honour promises of confidence or to avoid unnecessary embarrassment.

Every effort has been made to ensure the accuracy of the information provided but we accept sole responsibility for any errors or omissions.

The law is that at 30 September 1997.

Acknowledgements

We are indebted to David Longbottom who, when executive director of the Periodicals Training Council, identified the need for a practical guide such as this and on whose original idea the book is based. Vivien James, its first publisher, whose enthusiasm for the project persuaded Blueprint, an imprint of Chapman & Hall, to back it, was also greatly encouraging. Joanne Butcher, at the PTC, and Rebecca Barden, senior editor at Routledge, inherited responsibility for the project before the halfway stage and have been eager to steer it to completion. Kieran Dowling, from the Department of Employment, gave the project the Department's blessing and promise of financial support.

Wynford Hicks, Jenny McKay and John Morrish, industry professionals, read some of the early chapters and their constructive criticisms and comments have been incorporated whenever possible. Their unanimous verdict in favour of publication provided a tremendous boost.

Over the years, though they could not have known it then, many people in numerous ways had already begun making contributions to a book which had not even been thought about, that to name them all would be like publishing another telephone directory. Nevertheless, we hope they recognise their contributions in much of the content and we offer them collectively our gratitude and best wishes.

Journalists from magazine companies who attended media law courses helped to shape and test the practical aspects of those sessions, and among them we thank those from Benn Publications, BBC Magazines, EMAP Publications in London and Peterborough, Future Publishing, Haymarket, IPC Magazines, *Metal Bulletin*, Miller Freeman, PMA Training and its client companies, Reed Business Publishing, VNU and William Reed. Thanks also to journalists from Kent Messenger Group newspapers and to Reed Regional Newspapers in London and the Midlands.

Staffs of the training departments of those magazines and newspapers who invited us to conduct their media law training courses and whose efficient handling of the administrative arrangements ensured they ran smoothly also deserve our thanks.

Postgraduate students of periodical journalism at the School of Communication, University of Westminster, provided useful feedback as newcomers to the industry and we offer them our best wishes for happy and successful careers in magazines.

Extracts from reports and documents have been published by kind permission of the Periodicals Training Council; the Royal Society of Arts; the Press Standards Board of Finance (Pressbof), which finances the Press Complaints Commission; the National Union of Journalists; the Institute of Journalists; and the International Federation of Journalists.

The Schedule to the Defamation Act 1996 is Crown copyright.

Finally, we owe a special debt of gratitude to family, friends and colleagues whose tolerance, patience and understanding throughout the project has been unstinting.

An outline of the English legal system

1

INTRODUCTION

It is unlikely that the majority of journalists working on magazines will spend much, if any, of their working hours in the courts, but the time spent in acquiring an outline knowledge and understanding of the legal system is essential if they are to avoid 'howlers' and understand the legal copy they might be handling.

THE DIVISIONS OF THE LEGAL SYSTEM

There is widespread misunderstanding about the nature of the English legal system. That is why property owners often put up notices warning 'Trespassers will be prosecuted', which is a legal nonsense and unenforceable. Most trespasses are a civil law wrong (or tort) and prosecution is a criminal law procedure and the two are not interchangeable.

Historically, the legal system has developed two branches: criminal and civil, each with its own personnel, language and procedures. Although some crimes can also result in actions for damages (for example, a driver convicted of a traffic offence in the criminal courts could also face a claim for compensatory damages by an injured person in the civil courts), each case will be proceeded with independently, with its own rules of procedure.

THE CRIMINAL COURTS (see Figure 1.1)

MAGISTRATES' COURTS

Magistrates are either qualified lawyers and are known as stipendiary (i.e. salaried magistrates), or lay people without necessarily any legal qualifications.

Of all criminal cases, 99 per cent begin in the magistrates' courts and around 95 per cent of them end there. The odd 1 per cent are started by a

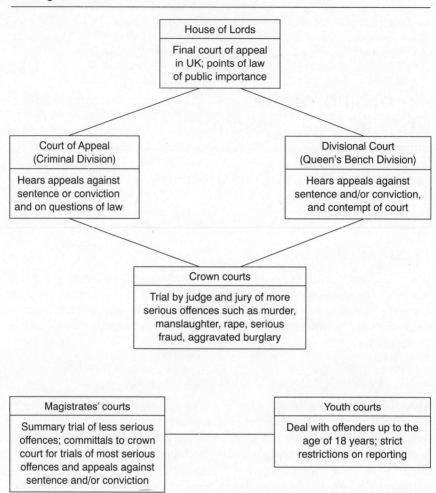

Figure 1.1 An outline of the criminal courts system

Bill of Indictment, a procedure which requires no preliminary investigation. Defendants charged with serious offences, such as murder, manslaughter, rape, robbery and driving offences causing death, have to be committed to the crown court for trial following a preliminary investigation to confirm that there is a case to answer. When this happens there are close restrictions, unless waived by the accused, on what can be reported, limiting stories to the accused's name, age, occupation and address, and details of the charge(s) against him or her. Reports should not include any evidence heard by the magistrates, only their decisions. Journalists should also remember that until the trial is over all the claims made against the accused are allegations and must be reported as such.

The procedure is quite simple. The prosecution, usually the Crown Prosecution Service, will outline the case against the accused to the magistrates and, if the accused pleads guilty, the defence will be allowed to plead mitigating circumstances with the hope of reducing punishment.

If the accused pleads not guilty, the prosecution will outline the facts of the case and call witnesses for the prosecution. These can be cross-examined by the defence. Then it is the turn of the defence to call witnesses on behalf of the accused, and these too can be cross-examined by the prosecution. When all the witnesses have been heard, the magistrates will retire to consider their verdict. They are advised on questions of law, not fact, by the court clerk. If they find the accused not guilty, he or she is free to leave the court. If, however, their verdict is guilty, they will hear evidence in mitigation of sentence from the accused's lawyer. The prosecution will also give details of any previous convictions. The magistrates will then announce sentence.

If a magistrates' court decides that its powers of sentence are too limited it will send the accused to the crown court for sentencing.

YOUTH COURTS

These used to be called juvenile courts but in 1991 they were renamed youth courts and are magistrates' courts that deal with crimes committed by children and young people up to eighteen years of age. They are not open to the public but journalists can attend. Again, there are firm restrictions on what can be reported and any material that is likely to identify the young person involved is not permitted. This includes a ban on publishing their names and addresses, the schools they attend and any photographs.

A youth court consists of justices chosen from a special panel. There must be three lay justices and at least one of them must be a woman.

CROWN COURTS

The crown court system was set up in 1972 to replace assizes and quarter sessions. The Central Criminal Court (or Old Bailey) is a crown court. They try all serious offences such as murder and attempted murder, manslaughter, rape and attempted rape and other sexual offences, major fraud, aggravated burglary and some wounding offences.

Trial is by judge and jury unless the defendant pleads guilty; there is then no need for a jury. The procedure is similar to that in magistrates' courts although often more formal. The judge rules on questions of law and passes sentence but the jury decides guilt or innocence. Juries are encouraged to reach unanimous verdicts but can arrive at majority verdicts if unanimity has proved impossible. The minimum ratio is 10–2 for a guilty verdict.

The crown court also hears appeals against sentence and/or conviction from magistrates' courts.

THE HIGH COURT

The criminal jurisdiction of the High Court is carried out in the Queen's Bench Division and is concerned with appeals from magistrates' and crown courts and with other matters such as writs for habeas corpus. High Court judges usually preside over the most serious criminal trials, sitting in crown court buildings.

THE COURT OF APPEAL (CRIMINAL DIVISION)

Appeals against sentence and/or conviction can also be heard by the criminal division of the Court of Appeal though these are usually restricted to questions of law rather than of fact. This court also is involved in appeals relating to contempt of court, and is staffed by Lord Justices of Appeal.

THE HOUSE OF LORDS

The highest court of appeal in the United Kingdom is the House of Lords. Hearings are concerned solely with cases involving questions of law of public importance.

THE CIVIL COURTS (see Figure 1.2)

MAGISTRATES' COURTS

Although the bulk of the work carried out in the magistrates' courts involves criminal proceedings they do have a limited amount of civil jurisdiction, particularly relating to family matters, neighbourhood quarrels, keeping the peace and binding over to keep the peace.

Panels of specially appointed magistrates sit as family proceedings courts, dealing with issues of welfare, custody, maintenance and adoption of children and access. They also act as licensing justices.

COUNTY COURTS

County courts have existed since 1846, but their jurisdiction has nothing to do with counties as such. They deal with cases involving contracts and other civil matters where the sum of damages being claimed is less than £50,000. Their jurisdiction is being constantly enlarged. In 1995 certain patent cases were referred to county courts. The Small Claims courts are part of the county courts and deal with claims for under £3,000. Their purpose is speed and informality. Generally the parties have to meet their own costs, including those of their solicitors.

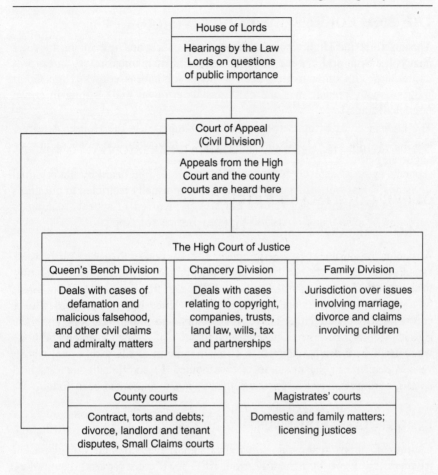

Figure 1.2 An outline of the civil courts system

THE HIGH COURT

The High Court has three divisions and unlimited jurisdiction, and is staffed by High Court judges. Chancery Division judges hear cases relating to copyright, companies, trusts, land law, wills, tax and partnerships. The Family Division has jurisdiction over issues involving marriage, divorce and claims involving children, and admiralty matters, hence the old slogan: Wives, Wills and Wrecks.

Journalists who are involved in actions for defamation or for malicious falsehood will find themselves appearing in the Queen's Bench Division, where most serious civil claims are heard.

THE COURT OF APPEAL (CIVIL DIVISION)

Appeals from the High Court and the county courts are heard here. It is the final court of appeal for the granting or refusal of injunctions.

THE HOUSE OF LORDS

The highest court of appeal in the United Kingdom is the House of Lords, hearings by the Law Lords are concerned solely with questions of law of public importance.

OTHER COURTS AND TRIBUNALS

CORONERS' COURTS

Although the power of coroners' courts is now weaker than when they were established in 1194, they still have an influential part to play in matters relating to deaths other than by natural causes. Any death that is sudden, unexplained or unnatural or that occurs as a result of violence has to be reported to a coroner. Coroners are either lawyers or doctors, and sometimes both, and their role is to hold inquests to determine the identity of the dead person and how, when and where death occurred. A coroner sometimes sits with a jury, whose verdict determines the outcome of the inquiry. In addition to inquests into deaths, coroners also determine whether or not treasure has been found.

INDUSTRIAL TRIBUNALS

Claims of unfair dismissal, for redundancy payments and compensation payments are heard by industrial tribunals. They are not 'courts' though they do have quite extensive powers. They deal also with cases of sexual and racial discrimination. They are usually open to the press and the public. Other tribunals include the lands tribunal, industrial injuries board, pensions board and tax commissioners.

THE LEGAL PROFESSION

SOLICITORS

The legal profession is dual in nature; lawyers are either solicitors or barristers though occasionally both, but can pursue only one or other profession at any one time. Although the distinction is becoming increasingly blurred, in general terms solicitors, with whom the public deals directly, tend to handle non-litigious matters such as conveyancing and the drafting of wills and administration of estates. They are instructed by their clients directly and do not have a general right of appearance in all the courts. They are controlled by the Law Society.

BARRISTERS

Barristers are known as counsel and spend most of their time advising on points of law or as advocates in the higher courts, where they have a partial monopoly and appear in wigs and gowns. Solicitor advocates wear gowns but not wigs. Barristers are not employed by the public directly but through a solicitor. After being 'called to the Bar' they are responsible for their professional conduct to the Inn of Court which has called them.

THE LAW OFFICERS

THE ATTORNEY GENERAL

The Attorney General is a Queen's Counsel (QC) and the government's chief legal officer. He is a politician as well as a lawyer and a member of the ruling political party. Normally his permission has to be sought to start proceedings for contempt of court, treason and other serious constitutional issues.

THE LORD CHANCELLOR

He also is a politician, a member of the Cabinet of the governing party and is appointed by the Prime Minister. The Lord Chancellor is head of the judiciary and Speaker of the House of Lords.

DIRECTOR OF PUBLIC PROSECUTIONS

This office-holder is a civil servant, not a politician, and heads the Crown Prosecution Service, whose role is to bring prosecutions on behalf of the Crown, having first consulted and advised the police on such matters as the evidence and the strength of the case.

It's a matter of reputation

2

INTRODUCTION

All people are entitled to their reputations whether they are good, bad or indifferent, and the laws of defamation exist to protect such reputations from unjustified or unwarranted attacks. Consequently it is vitally important that every journalist, whether working as a freelance or as a member of staff, whether as a writer or a production specialist, has a thorough knowledge and understanding of what such laws provide and how they can influence a journalist's day-to-day activities.

The real skill in journalism does not show simply in the cleverness of the ways of defending an action for defamation once it has been published, but in recognising a possible problem *before publication*, and then in handling it in such a way that any complaint after publication can be successfully rebutted or defended.

The maxim should be: 'If in doubt find out' rather than 'If in doubt leave it out', because a great deal of potentially damaging but justifiable public interest journalism can be published once the possible legal pitfalls have been recognised and avoided.

The law seeks a balance between a person's right to defend his reputation on the one hand and the defence of the freedom of speech and expression on the other.

WHAT IS A DEFAMATORY STATEMENT?

There is no one adequate and comprehensive definition of words or pictures that are defamatory, and journalists must consider the explanations used by judges when addressing juries over the past hundred years or more to glean from them the kinds of statements that are likely to be considered injurious.

The basic definition was given by a judge in 1840 when he described a defamatory statement as:

A publication . . . which is calculated to injure the reputation of another by exposing him to hatred, contempt or ridicule.

Since that time other judges have developed and elaborated on this definition. In 1924 Lord Justice Scrutton said that words

may damage the reputation of a man as a business man, which no one would connect with hatred, ridicule, or contempt.

In 1934 the same judge referred to words by Mr Justice Cave in 1882, who said:

The law recognises in every man a right to have the estimation in which he stands in the opinion of others unaffected by false statements to his discredit.

In general it is now accepted that a defamatory statement is one which does one or more of the following things:

● holds a person up to hatred, ridicule or contempt; or
● causes a person to be shunned or avoided; or
● disparages a person in his or her office, profession or trade; or
● tends to make right-thinking people, i.e. the jury, think less of a person.

Clearly allegations that imply dishonesty, immorality or other conduct that reflects adversely on a person's character will be defamatory.

Journalists must remember, too, that words might be defamatory of a company or a business or professional person even though they do not impute any moral blame.

To write that an architect has no aptitude for design or that an accountant has no mastery of arithmetic, for example, would be defamatory of them but not of others whose businesses did not require them to have such skills.

Companies can sue for libel in statements that damage their trading reputations. Individual employees of those companies also could bring actions in their own names.

THE DIFFERENCES BETWEEN LIBEL AND SLANDER

The law of defamation is divided into two parts: libel and slander. In simple terms, a libel is a defamatory statement published in permanent form, such as in a magazine or newspaper or on television or radio; a slander is a defamatory statement published by word of mouth, other than in a broadcast, for example during an interview.

Clearly the law of libel is the more dangerous for journalists because, once a statement has been published, it is there for anybody to read at any time and anywhere. Slander can be less hazardous because once the words have been spoken they are gone and, unless the defamatory allegations are made in the hearing of witnesses, they can be extremely difficult to prove.

This does not mean that journalists need not fear that actions for slander may be taken against them. In October 1994 the then Home Secretary Michael Howard was reported to have issued a writ for slander against the *Financial Times* after a telephone call between a reporter from the newspaper and a spokesman in the Home Office press department. Such action was initially denied by the Home Office but later was reported to have been confirmed by Mr Howard's solicitors.

Such actions make it clear just how dangerous it can be for journalists investigating defamatory allegations who have to rely on information from third parties because they cannot contact directly the person against whom the allegations are being made.

WHAT DOES A PLAINTIFF HAVE TO PROVE?

To be successful in an action for libel a plaintiff has to prove three things:

1   that the words were defamatory of him or her;
2   that the statement was reasonably understood to refer to the plaintiff; and
3   that they were published to a third person.

Publication to a third person is not a problem with libel because the words are there for anybody to read unless in a truly private or confidential communication.

A QUESTION OF IDENTITY

Identification needs careful consideration. Journalists cannot escape libel laws simply by not naming the people they are criticising. The test is whether the plaintiff has been identified in some way, and this does not always mean by name.

In 1981 the *Daily Telegraph* claimed that the description 'a wealthy benefactor of the Liberal Party' did not identify Mr Jack Hayward, but their argument was not accepted because the Liberal Party did not have many men who fitted that description and evidence was provided to show that the identification had been made.

It is also possible to identify people as members of a group or class of people.

Four journalists successfully sued the *Spectator* after the magazine had described them in a diary page piece as 'beer sodden hacks'. They had not been named but were described as belonging to a small group of journalists working at the Old Bailey.

Ten detectives won substantial damages from the *News of the World* after claiming they had been identified in a news story stating that some unnamed detectives from the CID in Banbury, Oxfordshire, where they were stationed, had raped a woman.

In 1981 the *Daily Mail* argued that the content of an article about the Unification Church (the Moonies) did not libel its UK leader Mr Dennis Orme, because he had not been named or alluded to in any way. But Mr Justice Comyn rejected that argument and held that the material was capable in law of being regarded as referring to Mr Orme.

There is an added danger, of course, that attacks on unnamed people can unintentionally libel others at whom the statement was not directed if they can show, nevertheless, that they have been identified.

The standard test of whether the words complained of are defamatory is that of the right-thinking member of society. This is not a particularly helpful definition for journalists and best practice is to think in terms of the magazine's readers.

Additionally, people's attitudes change over time; what might have been considered defamatory fifty years or so ago might not be regarded as such in the late 1990s.

WHAT THE PLAINTIFF DOES NOT HAVE TO PROVE

Unlike all other criminal and civil law actions where the burden of proof rests with the prosecution or the plaintiff, in an action for defamation the great weight of proof rests with the defendant.

In actions for libel, plaintiffs do not have to prove that allegations are false, nor that journalists intended to defame them. Nor are they required to prove they have suffered special (monetary) damage, because that will be presumed.

However, the situation is rather different in an action for slander where plaintiffs have to prove special damage except in cases where the allegation is one of the following:

1 they have committed a criminal offence punishable by imprisonment; or
2 have a contagious disease; or
3 a woman is accused of unchastity or adultery; or
4 where the allegation is calculated to disparage plaintiffs in their office, profession, calling, trade or business which they hold at the time of publication.

WHO CAN BE SUED?

In the past, as a general rule everybody who was responsible for publication of a libel could be sued, from writer to newsagent.

However, the Defamation Act 1996 states that a person has a defence to the proceedings if it can be shown that:

1 the person was not the author, editor or publisher of the statement complained of;
2 he or she took reasonable care in relation to its publication; and

3   did not know, and had no reason to believe, that what he or she did caused or contributed to the publication of a defamatory statement.

The Act further clarifies the meaning of 'author' as the originator of the statement, but does not include a person who did not intend that the statement be published at all, for example, if it is written in a private diary.

'Editor' is defined as a person having editorial or equivalent responsibility for the content of the statement or the decision to publish it; and 'publisher' is defined as a commercial publisher whose business is issuing material to the public and who, as part of that business, issues material containing the defamatory statement.

Exceptions protect people who are involved only in printing, producing, distributing or selling printed material containing the statement; in film or sound recording processing; in processing, making copies of, distributing or selling any electronic medium in or on which the statement is recorded, or in retrieving, copying or distributing such material.

Protection extends also to live broadcasts where the broadcaster has no effective control over the person making the defamatory statement, and to operators or providers of access to communications systems by means of which the statement is transmitted, or made available, by a person over whom the operator or provider has no effective control.

Employees or agents of an author, editor or publisher are in the same position as their employers if they are responsible for the content of the statement or the decision to publish it.

The law will take into account, in determining reasonable care, the extent of a person's responsibility for the content of the statement or the decision to publish it; the nature or circumstances of the publication; and the previous conduct or character of the author, editor or publisher.

OTHER CHANGES IN THE DEFAMATION ACT 1996

Changes in the Act are largely procedural rather than substantive. That means they are concerned with the handling of legal matters once a writ has been issued rather than with making any changes to the guidelines on defamatory statements as such.

AN OFFER TO MAKE AMENDS

One of the most significant changes is the introduction of an offer to make amends. Such an offer must:

1   be in writing;
2   be expressed to be an offer to make amends under Sec. 2 of the Defamation Act 1996

3   state if it is a 'qualified offer' (i.e. in relation to a specific defamatory meaning which the journalist accepts the statement conveys).

The offer is to:

1   make a suitable correction of the statement complained of and a sufficient apology;
2   publish the correction and apology in a manner that is reasonable and practicable in the circumstances; and
3   pay compensation (if any) and costs.

However, such an offer must be made *before* you serve a defence. The offer may be withdrawn before it is accepted, but if renewed it becomes a new offer.

If the offer is accepted, defamation proceedings end but the plaintiff is entitled to enforce the offer.

If you cannot agree with the plaintiff the steps which are to be taken by way of correction, apology and publication, you can make the correction and apology by a statement in open court and also give an undertaking to the court as to how it will be published.

Any disagreement on the amount of compensation to be paid will be settled by the court on the same principles as damages in defamation proceedings.

The court will look at the suitability of the correction, the sufficiency of the apology and whether the way it has been handled was reasonable in the circumstances. It has the power to increase or reduce compensation.

The court also has power to settle any disagreement about costs.

FAILURE TO ACCEPT AN OFFER

If an offer to make amends is made but not accepted, it is a defence unless:

1   you knew or had reason to believe that the statement complained of either did or was likely to be understood to refer to the plaintiff;
2   the statement was both false and defamatory of the plaintiff.

There is a presumption that you did not know points 1 and 2 above until it is proved to the contrary.

You can use the offer in mitigation of damages even if it was not used as a defence.

TIME LIMIT REDUCED

The time limit for bringing actions for defamation (and malicious falsehoods) is reduced from three years to one year, although the courts have a discretion to extend that period in special circumstances.

FAST-TRACK SUMMARY PROCEDURE

The court may dismiss the plaintiff's claim if it believes there is no realistic prospect of success and no reason why it should be tried.

Among issues to be taken into account are the seriousness of the alleged libel regarding content and extent of publication and whether a full trial is justifiable in the circumstances.

Alternatively the court may give judgment to the plaintiff and grant summary relief up to £10,000 where there is no defence to the claim which has a realistic prospect of success and there is no other reason why it should be tried.

The court can also order you to publish a suitable correction and apology and refrain from further publication of the offending copy. You should attempt to reach agreement with the plaintiff on the content of any correction and apology and the time, manner, form and place of publication.

If you cannot agree on the content the court can order you to publish a summary of its judgment. It can also tell you what to do in circumstances where you cannot agree on the time, manner, form or place of publication.

Summary proceedings are heard without a jury.

EVIDENCE OF CONVICTIONS

Proof that a plaintiff has been convicted of an offence is conclusive evidence that he or she committed that offence so far as it is relevant to the issue in question.

EVIDENCE CONCERNING PARLIAMENTARY PROCEEDINGS

Members of Parliament involved in defamation proceedings can now waive the protection which prevents the courts from questioning Parliamentary proceedings. This would have applied in the libel action brought by MP Neil Hamilton against the *Guardian* newspaper over cash-for-questions allegations if the action had not been withdrawn.

REPORTING COURT PROCEEDINGS

The Act gives the statutory protection of absolute privilege to the reporting of court proceedings provided such reports are fair and accurate, are published contemporaneously and the proceedings were open to the public. Until now such privilege had been only presumed, though widely accepted.

REPORTS PROTECTED BY QUALIFIED PRIVILEGE

Some reports covered by Schedule 1 Parts I and II (given in full at the end of Chapter 5) are protected by qualified privilege unless:

1 publication was made maliciously;
2 (for Part II) you were asked by the plaintiff to publish in a suitable manner a reasonable letter or statement by way of explanation or contradiction and you refused or neglected to do so.

The Act defines 'in a suitable manner' as in the same manner as the publication complained of or in a manner that is adequate and reasonable in the circumstances.

It does not protect publication of material which is not of public concern and publication of which is not for the public benefit. In this case the 'public' would be your readers.

UNINTENTIONAL DEFAMATION

Some limited protection might be provided for journalists who unintentionally publish defamatory statements, for example in a magazine serialisation or extract from a novel in which an allegedly fictitious character has some attributes that bear a close resemblance to a real person by name, lifestyle, profession, geographical location or some other detail.

The journalist should be able to show that the allegedly defamatory words were published innocently and without malice and that an offer of amends was made as soon as practicable.

FOREIGN PUBLICATIONS

The laws of defamation in foreign countries vary a great deal and discussion of them is outside the scope of this book. Journalists whose publications are distributed overseas should make sure that they do not publish any material that would be regarded as defamatory in those countries. The book *Carter-Ruck on Libel and Slander*, listed in the bibliography, gives a detailed analysis of the law of defamation in other countries.

AWARDS OF DAMAGES

Magazines which are successfully sued for libel will be required to pay a sum of money in damages; in general terms, these will be compensatory for injury to the plaintiff's reputation but not as a punishment against the magazine, or exemplary or punitive. In the latter case such damages might be awarded against a magazine if the court accepted that the publisher had considered the prospect of making a profit out of publication far outweighed any losses that might be sustained.

The amount of the award of damages will be fixed by a jury. Jury decisions became notorious with an award of £1.5 million in one case and just under that figure in another.

In 1988 a jury awarded damages of £300,000 against *Stationery Trade News*, a magazine with a circulation of around 9,000 a month, over allegations of counterfeiting and marketing products with misleading names.

Until 1995 juries in libel trials were given little if any guidance on how to assess damages. This changed after one jury awarded a total of £350,000 to entertainer Elton John when he won his libel action against Mirror Group Newspapers. The Court of Appeal took the view, long held by the media, that it was offensive that a person should recover damages for injury to his or her reputation which were often greater than might have been received for being helplessly crippled.

Now the courts can give some guidance to juries on what would be regarded as an appropriate award in the particular circumstances of each case, though it must be added that such figures are not binding.

Subsequently the award against MGN noted above was reduced by the Court of Appeal to £75,000.

CRIMINAL LIBEL

Claims brought against magazines and journalists for criminal libel are extremely rare; in 1982 the Law Commission recommended it should be abolished but this has not happened. Historically, publication of a defamatory allegation was regarded as a criminal libel if it was thought likely to lead to a breach of the peace; it was dealt with as a criminal prosecution with the possibility of a fine and/or imprisonment.

Actions for criminal libel cannot be brought without the consent of a High Court judge, who must believe that the libel so seriously damages the complainant's reputation that the public interest cannot properly be served without instituting criminal proceedings.

In 1975 the late Sir James Goldsmith, the financier, began a prosecution for criminal libel against the satirical magazine *Private Eye* which, Sir James claimed, was trying to vilify him and connect him with Lord Lucan who was wanted for questioning in a murder investigation. The criminal libel proceedings were dropped after *Private Eye* withdrew the allegations and publicly apologised to him.

For a criminal libel prosecution to be successful it is not necessary to prove publication of the allegations to a third person but only to the person allegedly defamed by them.

There is no civil law libel of the dead, but there could be a prosecution in criminal law libel if it can be shown that the statement about the deceased was published deliberately to provoke living relatives to commit a breach of the peace or that they might do so.

CHECKLIST

Before publication:

- Have statements of criticism or allegation been checked for defamatory meaning under the guidelines set out above (pp. 8–9)?
- Would evidence supporting defamatory allegations be legally admissible in court and is it correctly filed away?
- Has consideration been given to the appropriate defence(s) available?
- Has legal advice been taken?

After publication:

- Has an offer of amends been made, if appropriate?
- Has an alternative settlement been agreed?
- Has the time limit for bringing a libel action been met?
- Has legal advice been taken?

'Of course it's true, but can we prove it?'   3

INTRODUCTION

Truth is a complete defence to an action for libel. It does not matter how distressing, hurtful or damaging the allegation might be; if it is true you can publish it. The two possible exceptions to this principle are convictions regarded as 'spent' under the Rehabilitation of Offenders Act 1974, details of which are set out at the end of this chapter, and cases of criminal libel (see p. 16). But even in such cases the defence of truth will be defeated only if the plaintiff can prove that publication was malicious; that there was no justifiable reason for reporting them; and that the journalist was simply being spiteful or had some other improper motive.

It is one of the anomalies of well-intentioned legislation, however, that no restrictions apply to the reporting of acquittals, and a magazine need not fear a writ for libel by doing so.

The editor of a magazine read by workers in the community and social services sector fought off a claim that publication of the spent conviction of a paedophile who had obtained a job which brought him into close contact with children was malicious. It was important that readers of the magazine should know of the man's appointment. To prove malice the man would have had to show that the editor had no other motive than deliberately to injure the man's reputation.

WHAT DOES JUSTIFICATION MEAN?

The defence is known to lawyers as 'justification' but journalists should regard it as 'truth'. It has been the case since 1829 that:

> The law will not permit a man to recover damages in respect of an injury to a character which he does not or ought not to possess.

But beware. The word justification has connotations of 'public interest'. It suggests that you can defend an action for libel by claiming that you published a defamatory statement about a person because you believed it was justified in the public interest. Not so. It is important to remember that public interest by itself is not a sufficient defence to a libel claim, although it does form an essential part of the defences of qualified privilege and fair comment, discussed later in this book (pp. 32–44).

Be careful, too, about reporting convictions that can never be spent because they fall outside the provisions of the Rehabilitation of Offenders Act and which happened in the dim and distant past. Not all people who get a criminal record in their youth continue their criminal behaviour in later life, and they are entitled to be judged on their reputations as they are now and not on what they were.

The defence of truth sounds simple but, of the many ways there are to defend a libel action, justification is the most difficult to sustain. The journalist has the burden of proving truth 'on a balance of probabilities', unlike a criminal trial where the prosecution has to prove guilt 'beyond all reasonable doubt'. But if the defamatory allegation is of a criminal nature the burden of proof is raised to that of a criminal standard.

Additionally, a journalist who persists with this defence, and who fails to prove it, faces the probability of paying aggravated damages. Truth should never be relied on as a sole defence unless there is ample evidence to prove it.

Truth is not a complete defence to an action for criminal libel, discussed later in this chapter (pp. 21–2). In such cases the journalist must satisfy the court that publication was also for the public benefit.

HANDLING RUMOUR AND SPECULATION

Often journalists come into possession of information from people who assure them that what they are being told is true, or they hear rumours and speculation about people and events which place them in a bad light. Prime Minister John Major threatened to sue two magazines (*New Statesman and Society* and *Scallywag*) after they published rumours about him which the *New Statesman* said were not true.

It is not enough to say that you believed it was true, or were told that it was true. You must be able to prove truth with evidence that is admissible in court and convincing to an often unsympathetic jury.

As Lord Devlin said in the Appeal Court in 1964:

> you cannot escape liability for defamation by putting the libel behind a prefix such as 'I have been told that . . .' or 'it is rumoured that . . .', and then asserting that it was true that you had been told or that it was in fact being rumoured . . . For the purpose of the law of libel a hearsay statement is the same as a direct statement, and that is all there is to it.

A budding pop musician threatened to sue a journalist for libel over a news story that the musician had breached his contract and disappointed hundreds of fans by failing to turn up at a dance hall to judge a competition and to perform.

It was true that the musician did not appear but it was not true that he was in breach of contract. He had come to an informal arrangement with the dance hall manager that he would visit the dance hall without a fee, as a gesture of goodwill and to promote his career, unless he received an engagement for which he was to be paid. That is what happened.

Unfortunately for the journalist, the dance hall manager was far from precise in the language he used and talked about a contract when there was none. The matter was settled with publication of an apology, a glossy picture of the musician and a more than favourable review of his latest record! And, no doubt, some loss of credibility for the journalist and his publication.

The editor of a women's interest magazine received a feature from a free-lance journalist in which a woman claimed her husband had left her to live with another man. The inference, therefore, was that he must be homosexual.

It was certainly the type of feature the magazine wished to publish, but when deciding whether to print it the editor had to assess whether an allegation that a man was homosexual was capable of being defamatory and, if it was, how it could be proved. Could the wife be believed? What were her motives for wanting to publicise such a story? Did the phrase 'live with' imply a homosexual relationship between the two men or did it merely mean that they were living at the same address or sharing accommodation on a friendly but not a sexual basis?

Furthermore, if the magazine published the feature and the man sued, could his wife be relied on to substantiate her claim and, if necessary, to give evidence in support of the magazine at the trial? Was there any independent evidence? Could the other man also sue for libel? The editor decided the only safe way to handle the feature was to repeat the wife's claim to the husband himself and, incidentally, avoid the risk of an action for slander by not repeating the allegation to anybody other than him.

IS PUBLICATION OF A DENIAL ENOUGH?

If a person in this situation denies the allegations it raises the question of whether it is safe to publish them if you also publish in the same piece a denial of them by the person defamed.

Such an approach has to be handled with great care, for while it is true that publication of a denial could help to reduce any damage to the plaintiff's reputation, running the story on a main news page under vigorous bold headlines and with the denial carried in one paragraph at the end of the story, as is the general practice, could give the jury the impression that you believe the allegations or rumour and not the denial of them. In this kind of story it is wise to include the denial either in the introduction or at least in the first two or three paragraphs.

It is really a question of context, as one judge explained in a case dating back to 1835:

> If in one part of the publication something disreputable to the plaintiff is stated, but that is removed by the conclusion, the bane and the antidote must be taken together.

But in later cases judges have been rather more cautious in their judgments and have expressed the opinion that such cases 'must be comparatively rare'. As one judge said:

> It is a question of degree and of competing emphasis ... It may be easier to arrive at an answer where the publication contains an express disclaimer ... or where the antidote consists in a statement of fact destructive of the ingredients from which the bane has been brewed.

This issue is also discussed later (p. 92) in relation to headlines, text and photographs in a case involving actors from the popular television series *Neighbours*.

It is a calculated risk, but your dilemma could be eased a little if you put the defamatory allegations to the person concerned and offer them a chance to reply, making clear that such a reply would be considered as consent to publication of the libel.

In practice, this is unlikely to be the case and you need something more than a quick off-the-cuff comment from them to satisfy that test. You should not assume that people who decline to comment on defamatory information about them, or who make any other response, are giving you consent to publish.

WHAT YOU HAVE TO PROVE

The defence of justification requires that you prove the truth of libellous statements in substance and in fact, though the Defamation Act 1952 went some way towards easing this burden by not requiring proof of every single fact:

> In an action for libel or slander in respect of words containing two or more distinct charges against the plaintiff, a defence of justification shall not fail by reason only that the truth of every charge is not proved if the words not proved to be true do not materially injure the plaintiff's reputation having regard to the truth of the remaining charges.

There is no such provision in the Defamation Act 1996.

You might also be called upon to prove the truth of any innuendo, imputation, hidden meaning or other inference behind the style in which even provably true facts are reported. The Defamation Act 1996 says that the court shall not be asked to rule whether a statement is arguably capable, as opposed to capable, of bearing a particular meaning or meanings attributed to it.

Words have a natural and ordinary meaning but can in some circumstances have a defamatory meaning to people who have specialist knowledge of facts or circumstances. A journalist wrote a news story claiming that a local councillor had received preferential treatment in a housing repair programme. Although the journalist could prove that the councillor had indeed received preferential treatment, the court decided that the story carried the imputation that the councillor had 'secured' that preferential treatment for himself and this could not be proven.

In 1959 the *Daily Mirror* published an article about Liberace, a very popular American pianist, and described him as 'the summit of sex, the pinnacle of masculine, feminine and neuter' and portrayed him as a 'deadly, winking, sniggering, chromium-plated, scent-impregnated, luminous, quivering, giggling, fruit-flavoured, mincing, ice-covered heap of mother love'. Liberace argued that the piece suggested he was homosexual even though the word was never used, and successfully sued the newspaper for libel. History subsequently proved that Liberace was homosexual after his former partner and chauffeur brought a 'palimony' claim against him; in 1987 Liberace died of Aids.

Provided you can prove the 'sting' of the libel it should not matter that one or more relatively unimportant facts are wrong. For example, to say that a man was involved in a bank raid in Birmingham on Wednesday when, in fact, the robbery took place on Monday is not likely to materially alter the fact of his bad reputation.

PRACTICAL PROBLEMS

The practical problems of successfully defending a libel action by pleading justification are enormous and no journalist should take such a decision lightly.

Hearsay evidence is not admissible in legal proceedings and you cannot base your defence on what somebody, perhaps over a pint in the Rose & Crown, told you was true. You must be satisfied that it is true and not merely exaggeration, supposition, assumption, malice or misunderstanding. Be convinced your source is not misleading you. Ask if they are prepared to make a sworn statement to substantiate what they have told you and are prepared to appear as witnesses at the trial.

Make sure that all your documentary evidence is of sound quality: notes are full, clear, dated and the notebook intact. Often a plaintiff will claim that he has been misquoted but you can attempt to rebut this if you can show that your notes were made either at the time or as soon as possible after the event and are unedited. Adding to, or erasing from, notes once you know a problem has arisen is at best foolish and at worst disastrous. On the other hand, if you can give your evidence in the witness box from a detailed contemporaneous note you are more likely to impress the jury with your honesty and veracity.

The same applies to tape recordings of interviews. The tape must be clear, unambiguous and without breaks, and you must be able to show that it has not been edited in any way.

To do this you can hand it to a solicitor and get from them a dated note to the effect that the tape, notebook or any other material has been in their possession since that time.

Transcripts of tapes are not admissible unless you can prove they are verbatim and accurate, so do not record over used tape until you are certain it will not be required in legal proceedings.

KEEPING MATERIAL

Under the Defamation Act 1996, anyone who wants to sue for libel has a year in which to issue the writ after the statement has been published, although the Act does give the court power to use its discretion to extend this period. Judges will take into account the length of, and reasons for, the delay by the plaintiff and whether once the fact had become known he or she acted promptly and reasonably. They also will consider whether relevant evidence is likely to be unavailable or to be less cogent than if the action had been brought in time.

This obviously has implications for the length of time any original editorial materials, including tape recordings and notebooks, are kept. A minimum time is twelve months and a period of eighteen months is preferable. Reporters and feature writers should also keep a hard copy printout of work processed on screen or handed to the sub-editors as a check against what was written and what was published to avoid responsibility for errors that might arise at the production stage.

HOW TO DEAL WITH WITNESSES

Credible witnesses who can give firsthand accounts to support your defence are invaluable, but relying on witnesses alone does present problems. It can take two years and longer for a libel case to get to trial and in that time witnesses may have died, moved home without trace, claim their memories of events has faded over time or simply refuse to get involved in legal proceedings.

Conversely there are some benefits to the journalist in all this. You can rely on facts that come to light after publication to support your defence and this might encourage other witnesses to come forward on your behalf. The legal proceedings before trial lead to 'discovery of documents,' when both sides have to provide each other with all the documents relevant to the action. If either party has something to hide they are more likely to want to reach a quick out-of-court settlement than pursue the action. If all this fails you can hope that your lawyer is persuasive enough and skilful enough to elicit from the plaintiff in cross-examination evidence that will support your defence of justification.

REHABILITATION OF OFFENDERS ACT 1974

This legislation allows some people with criminal convictions to be regarded as rehabilitated after a certain period of time and to regard their convictions as 'spent'. The periods required for rehabilitation are cut by half for offenders under eighteen years of age.

The specified periods are:

- *ten years*
  (a) prison sentence, youth custody or corrective training for more than six months but not more than two and a half years;
  (b) cashiering, discharge with ignominy or dismissal with disgrace from the armed services;
- *seven years*
  (a) prison sentence or youth custody for not more than six months;
  (b) dismissal from the armed forces;
- *five years*
  (a) sentence of detention for a conviction in service disciplinary proceedings;
  (b) a fine or any other sentence.

For sentences that apply to young offenders the specified periods are:

- *seven years*: borstal training or more than six months' detention in the armed services;
- *five years*: detention for more than six months but less than two and a half years;
- *three years*: detention or a custodial order for six months or less, or for detention in a detention centre.

Rehabilitation periods vary for less serious sentences, such as absolute discharge, probation, conditional discharge, attendance centre orders, custody in a remand home and secure training orders, and journalists should consult a professional lawyer or one of the textbooks mentioned in the bibliography for more details.

CHECKLIST

Before publication:

- Have you checked and double-checked your facts?
- Have you checked and double-checked your sources?
- Have you obtained written statements from witnesses?
- Are your notes, tape recordings and other materials complete, dated, unambiguous and safely filed away?
- Having written the story or feature, have you had it 'legalled' according to office procedure?

After publication, if a complaint arrives it is unwise to deal with it without seeking proper legal advice. Verbal complaints should be confirmed in writing before you react:

- Acknowledge any letter.
- Do not apologise – this might be taken as an admission of liability.
- Corrections should not be published without agreement on the wording and written assurance that they will be in full and final settlement of the claim and that the content does not libel a third party – the writer for instance.
- Promising to publish a follow-up story to put the record straight is not recommended; it only complicates the issue.
- Hand all documentary evidence in your defence to your lawyer.
- Requests from the complainant for publication of a letter should be referred to your lawyer.

Handling court copy

4

INTRODUCTION

Magazines that carry news are likely to be faced from time to time with stories that relate to crimes allegedly or actually committed by their readers or that involve their readers as witnesses or victims or that are of interest to the readership. The main danger areas to be aware of are contempt of court and defamation. Contempt will arise when magazines publish evidence that has been ruled inadmissible or which has been heard in the absence of a jury; actions for libel can arise out of statements made by people who are not directly involved in legal proceedings or in follow-up interviews.

Although some magazine journalists might have experience in covering court proceedings, it is a fact that the vast majority of court stories appearing in magazines are submitted not by staff writers but by freelance journalists and law reporting agencies.

In February 1996 the Lord Chief Justice, Lord Taylor of Gosforth, told a London conference of journalists that much coverage of trials and sentencing was 'disappointing' and that some press reports were based on 'incomplete or slanted versions of the facts'.

It is vital, therefore, that any magazine journalist whose job it is to handle court copy provided by outside contributors should be familiar with the forms and rules of reporting if serious and damaging errors are to be avoided.

First, it cannot be emphasised too strongly that it is unsafe and unwise to publish court copy supplied other than by reputable freelance or agency contributors. Enthusiastic 'amateurs' keen to see their cases making the news will often submit copy that falls far short of what is legally required if it is to be published safely. Because of their personal involvement and their wish 'to put the record straight', they will concentrate on just their side of the story, taking little if any notice of the other side of the argument or reporting it in such a way that it presents a gross distortion of what actually took place in court. The danger is that inaccuracy or lack of fairness in the copy can be so serious that it becomes difficult, if not impossible, to defend what has been published in any legally recognised way.

Press officers in some local authorities and trade associations who are keen to gain publicity for their employers' legal successes in court will send reports of such cases to magazines in the hope that they will be published. It must be remembered, however, that such material is not completely protected by privilege and any inaccuracies in the published copy could be hard to defend.

WHAT PROTECTION IS PROVIDED?

Justice requires that people involved in legal proceedings should be free to tell the truth; that means: free from any threat of an action for defamation arising out of what they say in court. The protection is privilege and it applies to judges, magistrates, lawyers and witnesses, indeed to any person who is part of the proceedings. It does not apply to any interruptions by visitors in the public gallery, for example expressions of disbelief of witnesses or disparaging remarks against lawyers – however newsworthy they might be – nor does it apply to anything that might be said by a party to the proceedings in follow-up interviews.

The protection was originally provided by the Law of Libel Amendment Act 1888 which says:

> A fair and accurate report in any newspaper of proceedings publicly heard before any court exercising judicial authority shall, if published contemporaneously with such proceedings, be privileged; provided that nothing in this section shall authorise the publication of any blasphemous or indecent matter.

The 1888 Act did not specifically rule that the privilege was 'absolute', though that has always been assumed to be the case. Now the Defamation Act 1996 confirms that the privilege is absolute. The same privilege also protects statements made by MPs and members of the House of Lords during Parliamentary debates though reports of these by journalists receive only qualified privilege.

REQUIREMENTS FOR ABSOLUTE PRIVILEGE IN COURT REPORTS

It is clear, therefore, that such protection would apply to court proceedings published in magazines provided they meet the requirements of absolute privilege: that reports are fair, accurate, published contemporaneously and that the proceedings were open to the public. If they do meet them, then absolute privilege provides a bar to any action for defamation regardless of whether or not the allegations are true and no matter how offensive or damaging they might be.

Fairness

This means balance: the published report must give equal treatment to both sides of the case. This is particularly important where the accused in a criminal court has pleaded not guilty but has been convicted or has even been acquitted. It does not mean 'equal' in terms of words or column centimetres published, but, for example, that where allegations have been made and rebutted such rebuttals have been reported fully.

Accuracy

This speaks for itself. Privilege is unlikely to be lost for minor inaccuracies such as the misspelling of a name or getting someone's age wrong. Wrongly reporting that defendants had pleaded guilty when they had not, or had been convicted when in fact they had been acquitted would be impossible to defend. To report that a man had been found guilty of rape when, in fact, he had admitted indecent assault would also be libellous and indefensible, as one editor discovered to his dismay.

Published contemporaneously

This means publishing the report in the first possible edition of the magazine. Court copy should not be 'carried over' from one edition to the next, so a weekly magazine, for example, should be reporting proceedings that took place during the previous week.

Open to the public

This is not usually a problem because the vast majority of court proceedings are heard in public. It obviously does not apply to cases heard 'in camera', that is, in private.

HOW TO AVOID SOME COMMON PITFALLS

It is important to remember that, until a verdict has been reached, all claims made by the prosecution in a criminal case or by the plaintiff in a civil case are allegations and should be reported as such. Care must also be taken with head-lines (this is dealt with in more detail in Chapter 13). The intro on all court copy where cases are still proceeding should make it clear that it is a report of legal proceedings and any statement made should be attributed, for example by such phrases as 'a court was told', 'the prosecution claimed', 'a libel jury heard'.

Do not be so selective with the evidence published that the report loses its 'fairness'. Not all witnesses have to be reported but allegations denied in cross-examination should be included.

Evidence should be reported in the order in which it was given at the trial. When handling the report of a completed trial do not attempt to mix allegation and denial as though it were a routine news story. This could affect the overall balance of the report by giving undue emphasis to certain parts of it or even by inferring you believe a witness was lying.

Where reports are published before the proceedings have concluded, make sure that this is made clear at the end of the copy with a phrase such as 'the case continues'.

No reference should be made in news stories or features to people involved in current legal proceedings. In March 1996 a national daily tabloid was fined £10,000 for contempt of court after a sub-editor left references to the previous convictions of a woman on trial at crown court in a sports page story about her son. The judge accused the sub-editor of 'an act of crass incompetence'.

'INNOCENT' THIRD PARTIES

Sometimes witnesses giving evidence at a trial will make defamatory attacks on 'innocent' third parties, that is on people who are not part of the trial and who will not be in a position to respond in the witness box.

A former social worker on trial accused of sexually abusing children at a home he supervised claimed during his evidence that an MP had also abused children at the home. The MP was not part of the trial and was unable to deny the defamatory allegations until the trial had ended and the accused was in prison. The MP then made a statement in the House of Commons denying the claims.

A man accused of stealing jewellery from his former employer – a popular entertainer – denied the charges and said the entertainer had given him the jewellery in return for oral sex.

No action for slander could be taken against either of the men who had made the allegations because, whether they were true or false, as witnesses the evidence they gave was protected by absolute privilege. Journalists who wanted to report the allegations could do so without fear of being sued for libel because their reports also were protected by the same privilege, provided they met the requirements outlined above.

NO RIGHT OF REPLY

People who are the victims of such defamatory attacks often approach publishers to request a 'right of reply'. But no such right is available in those circumstances and care must be taken by editors who are minded out of a sense of fair play to provide complainants with an opportunity to tell their side of the story, because denials label the witnesses as liars and perjurers and could result in libel actions against editors. The complainant could seek permission to make a statement in open court and that, together with a journalist's report of it, would attract absolute privilege.

In the case cited above, the denial by the MP in the House of Commons was also protected by absolute privilege and no action for defamation could arise out of it or for fairly and accurately reporting it.

REPORTING RESTRICTIONS

Restrictions on what can be reported, particularly from criminal courts, mean that journalists who are handling court copy must be aware of possible errors by freelance journalists and court reporting agencies.

CHILDREN IN LEGAL PROCEEDINGS

Youth courts deal with offenders up to the age of eighteen years, who are entitled to anonymity. That means nothing can be published that would lead to their identification. Names, addresses and names of schools attended are not allowed, though ages can be mentioned, and no photographs can be used. In fact, there is a complete ban on publishing any material that would enable the young offender to be identified. This can present difficulties with relationships. Clearly to name the parent of a young offender would identify the youth.

There is no automatic ban on naming juveniles appearing as defendants or witnesses in adult courts though courts often issue orders under Sec. 39 of the Children and Young Persons Act 1933 forbidding identification – again a problem where relationships are involved.

MAGISTRATES' COURTS

Unless reporting restrictions have been lifted at preliminary hearings (and the copy should make it clear if they have), journalists are allowed to give an accused's name, age, occupation, address, the charge(s) and other relevant details but no evidence can be reported.

If an application for bail has been refused, the reasons should not be given because they are often prejudicial.

CROWN COURTS

The most common problem arising out of handling copy from crown courts is the reporting of evidence given in the absence of a jury. Editors have found themselves in contempt of court because they have reported that an accused has pleaded guilty to a number of offences but not guilty to others. Obviously the jury should not know about the guilty pleas: this is particularly important when a trial lasts for more than a few days.

In March 1996 a national daily newspaper was reported to the Attorney General, Sir Nicholas Lyell, for possible contempt of court proceedings after publishing details that had not been put before a jury at the Old Bailey in an arson case. The newspaper said one of its journalists did not realise until the trial was over that some material was not meant for publication. The Contempt of Court Act 1981 gives courts the power to order that publication of any report of court proceedings or part of those proceedings be postponed for as long as the court believes is necessary.

Sub-editors who are handling copy from magistrates and crown courts need to be particularly vigilant, therefore, to spot any obvious discrepancies and to check them out before publication.

IDENTIFYING VICTIMS OF SEX ATTACKS

People who claim that they have been victims of rape and other sexual offences are entitled to anonymity for life under the terms of the Sexual Offences (Amendment) Act 1992. The ban applies to men and women, boys and girls.

The offences include intercourse with a mentally handicapped person; indecent conduct towards young children; incitement to commit incest with a granddaughter, daughter or sister under sixteen; procurement of a woman by threats or by false pretences; administering drugs to obtain intercourse; intercourse with a girl under sixteen; procurement of a mentally handicapped person; incest by a man or woman; buggery; indecent assault on either a man or a woman; assault with intent to commit buggery.

Where an allegation has been made that one of these offences has been committed against a person, neither the name nor address can be published during the victim's lifetime. There is also a ban on publishing pictures.

Once a person has been accused of one or more of the above offences nothing can be published that would identify the accused. The restrictions can be lifted by a magistrate, or by a judge at crown court, if he or she is satisfied that such restrictions would make reporting the trial difficult and that lifting them would be in the public interest. Additionally the defence can apply to have the restrictions lifted to induce witnesses to come forward at the trial or on appeal. The identity of the accused can be revealed on conviction.

There is a defence to publication if you have the victim's written consent, provided it was obtained without unreasonable interference with the victim's peace or comfort.

CHECKLIST

● Is the copy properly attributed?
● Does the report meet the test for absolute privilege?
● Have all possible inaccuracies been checked?
● Is the identification of any juveniles legally safe?
● Are people who complain about sexual attacks unidentifiable, or do you have their written consent?

A degree of privilege

5

INTRODUCTION

Journalists have long argued that when they are carrying out bona fide legitimate investigative work their published reports should be protected by a statutory defence of public interest. That is not yet so and the Defamation Act 1996 has done nothing towards developing that defence as a general principle.

However, there are many occasions when journalists can safely publish defamatory information without fear of a successful libel action, provided they can show that their reports are protected by qualified privilege. The title of this chapter correctly indicates that this is not as strong a defence as that of absolute privilege discussed in the preceding chapter but it does provide a degree of protection to the publication of editorial material that otherwise would be difficult, because of problems of proof, for example.

COMMON LAW PRIVILEGE

The Common Law recognised that for the good of society in general there were occasions when one person should be free to make defamatory statements about another without fear of a writ. Of course, there are conditions that have to exist before the defence will apply. Many of the common law situations have been taken over by statutory provisions, first by the Defamation Act 1952 and now by the Defamation Act 1996.

The basis of the defence is that the person making the communication has an interest or a duty – legal, social or moral – to make it to someone who has a corresponding interest in it. This reciprocity is essential.

It is for a judge to decide whether any particular occasion is privileged. It is not sufficient that defendants honestly believe they were under a duty to speak. They must also honestly believe they were speaking the truth without any indirect or improper motive.

Because the audience is limited to those who have an interest in receiving the information it might be thought that, apart from the statutory provisions, it would not be available to magazines. However, it is available provided the circulation of the magazine is limited to people interested in the communication. This happened when *Retail Chemist*, a virtually controlled-circulation publication, published a reader's letter complaining about the trading activities of a supplier to the trade.

INFORMATION PROTECTED BY STATUTE

A detailed list of reports protected by qualified privilege is given at the end of this chapter, but in general terms it covers: legislatures, courts, international organisations and conferences worldwide; information issued by governmental departments of any member state of the European Union or the European Parliament, including the police; public meetings of local authorities and their committees; official commissions, tribunals and local inquiries; public meetings; general meetings of UK public companies, and appropriate circulated documents and reports of the findings or decisions of a wide range of cultural, business, sporting and charitable associations in the UK and other EU member states.

Part I of Schedule I of the Defamation Act 1996 (which is shown on pp. 36–9) sets out details of reports having qualified privilege without a requirement to publish an explanation or contradiction; Part II is a list of those statements which are protected by qualified privilege provided the publishers give the complainant an opportunity to explain or contradict them.

Unfortunately, Part II of the Schedule of the Defamation Act 1996 is less specific in some respects than the equivalent part in the Defamation Act 1952 (now repealed) in detailing the types of editorial material that qualify for protection. It leaves the decision in many cases to the Lord Chancellor in England, Wales and Northern Ireland or the Secretary of State for Scotland.

Nevertheless, the defence of qualified privilege will be especially valuable to parliamentary reporters and sketch writers, crime reporters, finance and business correspondents, and journalists covering the affairs of local government, provided always that the editorial material is of genuine public interest and is published for the public benefit. It excludes tittle-tattle gossip from whatever source and defamatory statements made by anyone outside protected proceedings. So, for example, remarks made by an MP during a debate in the House of Commons can be safely reported, even if those comments are defamatory, and the injured person has no opportunity to reply.

STATEMENTS NOT PROTECTED

Defamatory statements published in reports of follow-up interviews with the MP or the person he has criticised will not be subject to qualified privilege because they are made outside the protected proceedings.

Additionally, qualified privilege under the Act does not give any defence to reports of statements made by representatives of bodies such as National Health Service Trusts, transport authorities and other similar public sector organisations.

Information does not have to be in writing to qualify for protection; this is especially useful to journalists who have to carry out much of their investigative work on the telephone. But not everything said even by authorised spokespersons is automatically covered. This was clarified in a case in 1983 involving conversations between a *Daily Telegraph* reporter and a government press officer. Lord Justice Stephenson said that there was a difference between written information and that 'pulled out of the mouth of an unwilling officer of the department', and that not every statement of fact made to a journalist by a press officer of a government department is privileged. This rules out protection for journalists' own interpretations, gloss or comments on what they were told.

It also is important to remember that the defence of qualified privilege will be lost if reports are proven to have been published maliciously or are not fair and accurate.

RIGHT OF REPLY

People who have been subjected to criticism and abuse by journalists in magazine editorial often seek a right of reply and in doing so might defame others. This can be dangerous.

The defence of qualified privilege does go some way towards allowing editors to publish letters which deny allegations made against the writers, provided they are reasonable in tone. This was established by the House of Lords in the case of *Adam* v *Ward* in 1917 and followed by the Court of Appeal in 1995.

Adam, an MP, used his parliamentary privilege to criticise a general in his former regiment. Subsequently the Secretary to the Army Council issued a statement of support for the general which was widely published and which libelled the MP. The Law Lords ruled that, as the statement in the House of Commons had received tremendous publicity, it was a matter of justice that the rebuttal should also do so.

Similarly, in 1995 the Court of Appeal in the case of *Watts* v *Times Newspapers* followed this ruling. A Mr Nigel Watts claimed damages for libel in respect of material in *The Sunday Times*, some of which accused the plaintiff, an author, of plagiarism. Subsequently the newspaper published a letter from the plaintiff denying the allegations of plagiarism. Lord Justice Hirst said that Mr Watts had been the victim of an attack and had a right to reply in order to rebut the allegations against him 'and to do so with considerable degree of latitude, so long as he did not overstep the bounds and include entirely irrelevant and extraneous material'.

CHECKLIST

Before publication:

- Is your material covered by interest and duty?
- Is the libellous material protected by Part I or II of the Schedule to the Defamation Act 1996?
- Do all criticisms arise from protected proceedings?
- Are you sure that no comment in follow-up interviews is defamatory of other people?
- Is the journalist reporting privileged fact and not personal interpretation of it?
- Is the report fair and accurate and not published maliciously?

After publication:

- Are agreed apologies within the terms of the *Adam* v *Ward* case and have they been cleared by lawyers?
- Are statements in accordance with the right of explanation or contradiction?

DEFAMATION ACT 1996: SCHEDULES

SCHEDULE 1

QUALIFIED PRIVILEGE

PART I

STATEMENTS HAVING QUALIFIED PRIVILEGE WITHOUT EXPLANATION OR CONTRADICTION

1. A fair and accurate report of proceedings in public of a legislature anywhere in the world.

2. A fair and accurate report of proceedings in public before a court anywhere in the world.

3. A fair and accurate report of proceedings in public of a person appointed to hold a public inquiry by a government or legislature anywhere in the world.

4. A fair and accurate report of proceedings in public anywhere in the world of an international organisation or an international conference.

5. A fair and accurate copy of or extract from any register or other document required by law to be open to public inspection.

6. A notice or advertisement published by or on the authority of a court, or of a judge or officer of a court, anywhere in the world.

7. A fair and accurate copy of or extract from matter published by or on the authority of a government or legislature anywhere in the world.

8. A fair and accurate copy of or extract from matter published anywhere in the world by an international organisation or an international conference.

PART II

STATEMENTS PRIVILEGED SUBJECT TO EXPLANATION OR CONTRADICTION

9.—(1) A fair and accurate copy of or extract from a notice or other matter issued for the information of the public by or on behalf of—

(a) a legislature in any member State or the European Parliament;

(b) the government of any member State, or any authority performing governmental functions in any member State or part of a member State, or the European Commission;

(c) an international organisation or international conference.

(2) In this paragraph 'governmental functions' includes police functions.

10. A fair and accurate copy of or extract from a document made available

by a court in any member State or the European Court of Justice (or any court attached to that court), or by a judge or officer of any such court.

11.—(1) A fair and accurate report of proceedings at any public meeting or sitting in the United Kingdom of—

(a) a local authority or local authority committee;

(b) a justice or justices of the peace acting otherwise than as a court exercising judicial authority;

(c) a commission, tribunal, committee or person appointed for the purposes of any inquiry by any statutory provision, by Her Majesty or by a Minister of the Crown or a Northern Ireland Department;

(d) a person appointed by a local authority to hold a local inquiry in pursuance of any statutory provision;

(e) any other tribunal, board, committee or body constituted by or under, and exercising functions under, any statutory provision.

(2) In sub-paragraph (1)(a)—
'local authority' means—

(a) in relation to England and Wales, a principal council within the meaning of the Local Government Act 1972, any body falling within any paragraph of section 100J(1) of that Act or an authority or body to which the Public Bodies (Admission to Meetings) Act 1960 applies,

(b) in relation to Scotland, a council constituted under section 2 of the Local Government etc. (Scotland) Act 1994 or an authority or body to which the Public Bodies (Admission to Meetings) Act 1960 applies.

(c) in relation to Northern Ireland, any authority or body to which sections 23 to 27 of the Local Government Act (Northern Ireland) 1972 apply; and

'local authority committee' means any committee of a local authority or of local authorities, and includes—-

(a) any committee or sub-committee in relation to which sections 100A to 100D of the Local Government Act 1972 apply by virtue of section 100E of that Act (whether or not also by virtue of section 100J of that Act); and

(b) any committee or sub-committee in relation to which sections 50A to 50D of the Local Government (Scotland) Act 1973 apply by virtue of section 50E of that Act.

(3) A fair and accurate report of any corresponding proceedings in any of the Channel Islands or the Isle of Man or in another member State.

12.—(1) A fair and accurate report of proceedings at any public meeting held in a member State.

(2) In this paragraph a 'public meeting' means a meeting bona fide and lawfully held for a lawful purpose and for the furtherance or discussion of a matter of public concern, whether admission to the meeting is general or restricted.

13.—(1) A fair and accurate report of proceedings at a general meeting of a UK public company.

(2) A fair and accurate copy of or extract from any document circulated to members of a UK public company—-

(a) by or with the authority of the board of directors of the company,

(b) by the auditors of the company, or

(c) by any member of the company in pursuance of a right conferred by any statutory provision.

(3) A fair and accurate copy of or extract from any document circulated to members of a UK public company which relates to the appointment, resignation, retirement or dismissal of directors of the company.

(4) In this paragraph 'UK public company' means—

(a) a public company within the meaning of section 1(3) of the Companies Act 1985 or Article 12(3) of the Companies (Northern Ireland) Order 1986, or

(b) a body corporate incorporated by or registered under any other statutory provision, or by Royal Charter, or formed in pursuance of letters patent.

(5) A fair and accurate report of proceedings at any corresponding meeting of, or copy of or extract from any corresponding document circulated to members of, a public company formed under the law of any of the Channel Islands or the Isle of Man or of another member State.

14. A fair and accurate report of any finding or decision of any of the following descriptions of association, formed in the United Kingdom or another member State, or of any committee or governing body of such an association—

(a) an association formed for the purpose of promoting or encouraging the exercise of or interest in any art, science, religion or learning, and empowered by its constitution to exercise control over or adjudicate on matters of interest or concern to the association, or the actions or conduct of any person subject to such control or adjudication;

(b) an association formed for the purpose of promoting or safeguarding the interests of any trade, business, industry or profession, or of the persons carrying on or engaged in any trade, business, industry or profession, and empowered by its constitution to exercise control over or adjudicate upon matters connected with that trade, business, industry or profession, or the actions or conduct of those persons;

(c) an association formed for the purpose of promoting or safeguarding the interests of a game, sport or pastime to the playing or exercise of which members of the public are invited or admitted, and empowered by its constitution to exercise control over or adjudicate upon persons connected with or taking part in the game, sport or pastime;

(d) an association formed for the purpose of promoting charitable objects or other objects beneficial to the community and empowered by its constitution to exercise control over or to adjudicate on matters of interest or concern to the association, or the actions or conduct of any person subject to such control or adjudication.

15.—(1) A fair and accurate report of, or copy of or extract from, any adjudication, report, statement or notice issued by a body, officer or other person designated for the purposes of this paragraph—-

(a) for England and Wales or Northern Ireland, by order of the Lord Chancellor, and

(b) for Scotland, by order of the Secretary of State.

(2) An order under this paragraph shall be made by statutory instrument which shall be subject to annulment in pursuance of a resolution of either House of Parliament.

'In my opinion . . .'   6

INTRODUCTION

Everyone is entitled to express his or her opinion about any matter that concerns them. A meal in a restaurant, a book read, a play seen or a television documentary viewed are all vehicles which drive people to comment, sometimes favourably, sometimes not. In this respect journalists have no special privileges, but they do have an enormous advantage over other people: they can publish their opinions to the many millions of people who read magazines and newspapers, watch television and listen to the radio.

However offensive, outrageous or potentially damaging their opinions might appear to others to be, all can claim protection from actions for libel by the defence of fair comment. It is the defence used by critics, reviewers, leader writers, political commentators, parliamentary sketch writers, 'gossip' columnists and any other journalist whose job it is to express opinions about what people have done or not done, or have said or not said. Any matter of public interest is a fair target for comment – either in editorial columns or in readers' letters.

THE 'FAIR COMMENT' TEST

To establish a defence of fair comment journalists do not have to get opinion on their side. They should succeed so long as they can prove that their opinions are honestly held, that they are published without malice, are on a matter of public interest and that the facts on which the opinions are based are provably true or are published in privileged material, for example the report of a public inquiry which has the protection of qualified privilege.

WHAT DOES 'FAIR' REALLY MEAN?

The title 'fair comment' is misleading because comment does not have to be 'fair' in the normal and ordinary meaning of the word. It is better to think of the defence as 'comment' or 'opinion'.

This was aptly defined by Lord Esher in the case of *Merivale* v *Carson* in 1887, when he said:

> Every latitude must be given to opinion and to prejudice and then an ordinary set of men with ordinary judgment must say whether any fair man would have made such a comment. A mere exaggeration or even gross exaggeration would not make the comment unfair. However wrong the opinion expressed may be in point of truth or however prejudiced the writer it may still be within the prescribed limits.

And he went on:

> The question which the jury must consider is this: Would any fair man, however prejudiced he may be, however exaggerated or obstinate his views, have said that which this criticism has said?

This certainly gives columnists and critics what often has been described as a licence to publish 'unfair comment'. Indeed, in a case in 1942 another judge said:

> A critic is entitled to dip his pen in gall for the purpose of legitimate criticism; and no one need be mealy-mouthed in denouncing what he regards as twaddle, daub or discord.

THE ESSENTIAL DIFFERENCE BETWEEN FACT AND COMMENT

Fair comment provides a defence only to defamatory expressions of opinion and not to defamatory statements of fact. It is essential that readers should be able to distinguish between fact and opinion in a column or letter, and the material should be written in such a way that readers can say: 'These are the facts and these are the writer's comments on those facts'.

One restaurant critic wrote that a curry he had eaten was not 'hot', and subsequently, when the restaurateur threatened to sue for libel, much time and money was spent arguing whether this was a statement of fact and provably true or a statement of opinion.

Journalists do not have to persuade readers, or members of a libel jury, that the journalist's opinions are correct or true. Indeed, it is impossible to prove the truth of opinion. One useful device is to state the facts and then say, as in parenthesis, something like 'and in my opinion' or 'the *Traders' News* believes this to be . . .'.

Be careful not to turn defamatory statements of opinion into facts such as 'in my opinion he is a crook' or 'this magazine believes the company is racist'. You cannot pass off as comment allegations of criminal or immoral behaviour.

GET YOUR FACTS RIGHT

In whatever way opinion or comment is presented in a magazine, some reference must be made to the facts on which it is based, by reference in a leader column to a news story on another page, for example.

Journalists cannot succeed with a defence of fair comment on inaccurate information or where the facts are not clearly stated. However honestly and sincerely opinion is expressed on the reported facts, if they are incorrect fair comment will provide no protection. Nor will it cover instances where journalists have been selective with the facts in order to support a personal and particular point of view. This is tantamount to publication with malice.

A journalist strongly criticised former Tory Prime Minister Sir (then Mr) Edward Heath for failing in his duties and responsibilities to his constituents because he took part in too many non-parliamentary pursuits. The journalist told his readers how five other MPs in the area beavered away and regularly bombarded him with information and news stories about their activities, but went on:

> But from the sixth there is only silence. Never a telephone call or letter from him to this office, never an indication that he shows the slightest interest in what is going on in his own backyard.

The true facts were that in the year leading up to the time the opinion column was published Mr Heath, who did not live in his constituency, had been there, on business, on more than 150 occasions, and in the seven days leading up to the time of publication he had visited his constituency no fewer than eight times.

He claimed the allegations were the gravest and most disparaging charge on the integrity of a constituency MP, and the matter resulted in what must be the longest, most grovelling published apology in British legal history. It took the form of a letter from the MP which was in excess of 1,000 words and headlined as 'an apology for a malicious attack'.

Had the case gone to trial the test for the jury would have been: Could any fair minded person honestly express that opinion on the proven facts? The answer must surely have been no.

In June 1990 a leading magazine for the computer industry wrongly reported in a front page lead news story that the electrical safety of computers from five manufacturers, who they named, had been questioned in a report sent to the Department of Trade and Industry for investigation. The story claimed that more than one of a named company's range of personal computers failed the flashover test immediately upon power-up. And it warned: 'This means that a mains supply short circuit in the system could make the chassis go live, creating a risk of electrocution.' The report also contained other damaging facts about a number of other PCs.

The editor commented on this in a leader column under the heading: 'A shocking story of safety gone astray'. His column added: 'In recent years PC manufacturers have made strenuous efforts to rid themselves of their back-street bodger image. Now it seems that the industry's reputation for throwing products together without thought for design or safety is deserved.'

Unfortunately, there was no truth in any of the allegations in the news story, which had not been substantiated during enquiries, and the magazine was faced with publishing an apology and correction and, it is reported, a considerable loss of advertising revenue. The news story could not be defended by justification because there was no evidence that the allegations it made were true and, therefore, no matter how honest and sincere were the editor's feelings in writing his editorial, it could not be defended on the grounds of fair comment because it was based on inaccurate information. Even the most experienced journalists can make mistakes.

THE PITFALLS IN REVIEWING

Although one judge has said that critics need not be mealy-mouthed in denouncing poor-quality work, journalists cannot always rely on fair comment to get them out of trouble when faced with a libel action. Problems can arise when criticising people from the catering, entertainment, literary and arts worlds as well as when commenting on any company's activities.

In May 1989 Britain's *Caterer & Hotelkeeper* magazine published a news story from a correspondent in Australia, reporting that a A$30 meal had cost an Australian daily newspaper A$100,000 (£47,600) after the restaurateur had successfully sued the newspaper for libel. And it warned: 'The case could have serious implications for restaurateurs and critics in Britain.'

The critic described food at one Sydney restaurant as 'so overcooked it might have been an albino walrus served in a charred husk of a shell'. He reported that the lemon sole was 'a slab of overcooked fish, slimy with oil' and his garlic prawns were 'chewy little shapes'. The jury decided that the review had defamed the restaurant's *patron*. Although decisions in Australian courts are not binding in Britain, they are often said to be 'persuasive' because both countries share a common law system.

When (as referred to on p. 22) the American entertainer Liberace first came to Britain in the late 1950s, the *Daily Mirror* had a columnist who described him as 'the summit of sex, the pinnacle of masculine, feminine and neuter. Everything that he, she or it can ever want.' The article went on to describe the flamboyant entertainer as a 'deadly, winking, sniggering, chromium-plated, scent-impregnated, luminous, quivering, giggling, fruit-flavoured, mincing, ice-covered heap of mother love . . .'.

Liberace sued for libel on the grounds that the article suggested he was homosexual, because of the 'fruit-flavoured' description, and the jury rejected the newspaper's argument that it was defensible on the grounds of justification and fair comment. Many years later Liberace did die of an Aids-related illness after his former partner who was also his chauffeur had sued him for what amounted to a claim for unfair dismissal.

More recently, in 1985, the actress Charlotte Cornwell successfully sued the *Sunday People* and its television critic Nina Myskow over a review of the actress's performance as a rock-and-roll star in a TV series. As well as writing of the actress that 'her bum's too big', the review went on to say: 'She can't sing and she has the sort of stage presence that jams lavatories.' She also described her as middle-aged.

The argument in court was whether the comments were about the actress's performance or whether they were statements of fact. The jury at the first trial (there was a re-trial on appeal) clearly believed they were statements of fact and awarded the actress £10,000 damages. At the subsequent re-trial the jury must have been of the same opinion and awarded her slightly more – £11,500 in damages.

READERS' LETTERS

Care must be taken when publishing readers' letters in which they comment on facts that might not be stated in the letter or are not known to be true to the magazine's journalists or to its wider readership. People often write letters to magazines on some public issue out of personal spite or perhaps because they have a particular axe to grind.

Journalists must be able to determine when a reader is being honest and sincere and a check on the accuracy of the stated facts is a wise precaution before the letter is published. The natural journalistic instinct for 'a con' is invaluable here.

A magazine which receives a complaint arising out of publication of a reader's letter has the same defences as those that apply to allegedly defamatory news and feature articles. The additional burden in handling complaints about defamation in a reader's letter is that the magazine has the burden of proving the truth of the reader's facts before it can enter a defence of fair comment.

This does beg the question, of course, as to whether the editor can be said to share and support the opinion of the letter writer. The answer is Yes if the comment can pass the test stated above (p. 40), that is, that it is the kind of opinion that could be expressed by any fair-minded person.

The moral is that readers' letters must be checked for authenticity and accuracy very thoroughly before publication.

CHECKLIST

- Does the column pass the fair comment test?
- Are the facts clearly stated and provably true?
- Is fact clearly distinguishable from opinion?
- Has criticism in a reader's letter been checked for factual accuracy and malice?

When you put it to the test

INTRODUCTION

Magazines provide a valuable reader service by publishing product reviews and performance tests. The question that often arises is: How far can I go? There are three major considerations here: the editorial integrity of the content; the wish that no adverse criticism be published that would offend advertisers and cause them to withdraw their business, with subsequent loss of revenue; and the possible legal consequences of highly critical and, therefore, potentially damaging editorial coverage of a company's products.

The reputation of any publication in the eyes of its readers can determine its commercial health, but this demands a proper understanding and relationship between the editorial and advertising departments.

Journalists need to know the differences between libel and malicious falsehood and the legal concept of malice when writing product or performance test reports.

THE IMPACT OF THE *YACHTING WORLD* CASE

In the summer of 1994 the verdict in what is now widely referred to as the *Yachting World* case sent shock waves through the magazine publishing industry. The jury in a libel trial brought by Mr John Walker, his wife Jean and their company, Walker Wingsail Systems, against the magazine awarded the plaintiffs nearly £1.5 million in damages after deciding that a feature including a performance test report of the company's aerofoil-driven trimaran published in the magazine in February 1993 was libellous. It became the second-largest libel damages award in England.

The report compared and contrasted the manufacturer's claims for the performance of the trimaran with those found by the magazine's journalist who carried out the performance test. He also commented on the claim made by the company that it had attracted export deals worth nearly £2 million for its range of wingsail-powered yachts, but 'when pressed Walker would only confirm one order', the rest were in the form of 'returnable deposits'. The plaintiffs claimed that the article implied they were charlatans and liars.

The magazine appealed against the verdict and the case was resolved in an out-of-court settlement by payment to the plaintiffs of £760,000 in damages and costs.

The immediate result of the award was to cause publishing company managers to send out warnings to editors that they were not to carry critical product and performance test reports because of the danger of having excessive damages awarded against them. Even sections of the media business press believed that the trial result meant the end of product test reports as such. *UK Press Gazette* claimed in its edition of 26 September 1994 that 'Only reform will sink libel lottery'.

This panic served to show that there is often a fundamental misunderstanding of the many important differences between actions for libel and those for malicious falsehood, one of which is known as slander of goods, sometimes referred to as 'trade libels', by which complaints resulting from allegedly untrue and disparaging product reviews are judged.

THE DIFFERENCES BETWEEN LIBEL AND MALICIOUS FALSEHOODS

Libel actions are brought by individuals who claim unfair and unjustified attacks on their general reputations or by companies which argue damage to their trading reputations. Actions for slander of goods (the title itself is misleading because these slanders can be in print) are brought where the plaintiff claims the journalist has disparaged the company's goods or services in a malicious way, resulting in financial loss but not necessarily in loss of reputation. It is a fine line to draw but it is a vital one.

The distinction was best dealt with by Lord Esher in 1894 when, as the then Master of the Rolls in the case of *South Hetton Coal Co.* v *North-Eastern News Association*, he explained:

> Suppose the plaintiff was a merchant who dealt in wine, and it was stated that wine which he had for sale of a particular vintage was not good wine ... the statement would be with regard to his goods only, and there would be no libel ... On the other hand, if the statement was so made as to import that his judgement in the selection of wine was bad, it might import a reflection on his conduct of his business, and shew that he was an inefficient man of business. If so, it would be a libel.

Another Master of the Rolls said similarly that to disparage a trader's goods did not give an action for libel unless the words used imputed carelessness, misconduct or lack of business skill.

Lord Esher's opinion was regarded as persuasive in a case as comparatively recently as 1970. This helps to explain why the case against *Yachting World* was one for libel and not for slander of goods.

In an action for libel there has to be proof that the words are defamatory; this does not apply in actions for malicious falsehood. Once a statement has been proved to be defamatory there is a presumption that it is false and the journalist has to prove otherwise; in a malicious falsehood case the plaintiff has the burden of proving that the statement is untrue.

In a libel action the plaintiff does not have to prove that the journalist published a defamatory statement maliciously unless the journalist's defence is one of qualified privilege or fair comment; malice must be proved by the plaintiff in a malicious falsehood case.

Proof of special damage (such as financial loss) is not necessary in a libel action or where certain slanderous allegations are made because it is presumed in law; the plaintiff has to prove financial loss in cases of malicious falsehood.

The death of either party in a libel action ends the action; cases of malicious falsehood can be carried on by the deceased's personal representative.

Damages in a libel action usually include a monetary sum for injury to the plaintiff's feelings; this does not apply in cases of malicious falsehood where damages will be awarded only for monetary loss.

In actions for libel the plaintiff has a right to trial by jury unless the case involves technical or scientific considerations or its trial would be too onerous for a jury. The case brought by the fast-food chain McDonalds Restaurants is an example of such an exception. There is no jury in malicious falsehood cases.

To defend a case of malicious falsehood the journalist must be able to prove that he acted in good faith and without malice. An offer to publish a speedy correction where error is admitted will help to support this assertion.

SO HOW FAR CAN YOU GO?

Journalists who follow the simple guidelines set out below should feel able to publish critical product reviews with confidence:

- Be sure you have tested the manufacturer's product according to the instructions supplied with it; follow them to the letter.
- Be careful when making adverse comparisons between your test results and those of a comparable product or the manufacturer's own claims that you are really comparing like with like.
- Make sure you can prove the accuracy of your facts.
- If you get results significantly different from those claimed by the manufacturer, refer back to them *before* publication. This is evidence that you are at least trying to be fair.

Mr George Carman QC, acting for the plaintiffs in the *Yachting World* case, asked Mr Walker in the witness box:

This article contrasts what is in your literature with his [the journalist's] own findings. Did this professional journalist ever give you an opportunity to answer the attacks he was about to make on you?

To which Mr Walker replied: 'No. Never.'

It is a very powerful way of casting doubt on the professional integrity of the journalist and of suggesting lack of good faith, honest belief and confidence in what he or she wrote. Disagreement about the validity of the test and your subsequent criticism of the product could be used as evidence of malice if it can be shown that you did not genuinely believe what you wrote.

Make it clear whether what you are publishing is a product test or a performance test; if it is a performance test make clear the conditions under which the test was carried out. Many products, such as yachts, cars, motor cycles, lawnmowers, for example, perform variously under different conditions of weather, climate, surface and so on.

Do not criticise a product for not performing a task for which it was not intended or designed.

Some magazines often use testing panels made up of their own readers. There is nothing wrong with this but you must point out in the magazine how the panel was constituted. Try to avoid selecting a tester who, however fair-minded, could be shown to have an axe to grind, and declare the testers' qualifications.

OTHER TYPES OF MALICIOUS FALSEHOODS

Journalists can be sued for malicious falsehoods arising out of statements other than those contained in product and performance tests. Any false statement that is capable of being financially damaging and is made maliciously can lead to a claim for damages. Some errors can be shown to be simple honest mistakes and are speedily corrected. Others are not so easily dealt with. For example, to report wrongly that a company has ceased trading could lead to an action for malicious falsehood to recover the damage caused by customers finding other outlets to satisfy their needs.

In April 1996 Tory MP Rupert Allason, who also writes fiction under the name of Nigel West, claimed that some journalists and the *Daily Mirror* carried out a campaign to destroy the writer's reputation when, in 1992, the newspaper reported that fifty MPs had signed an early-day motion challenging Mr Allason to give to Maxwell pensioners an estimated £250,000 he had received in libel damages from a newspaper. The MP sued the journalists and the *Daily Mirror* for malicious falsehood.

Dismissing Mr Allason's claim, Sir Maurice Drake, sitting as a judge of the Queen's Bench Division, said the story had been false and had been published maliciously but Mr Allason had not been able to prove that he had lost a book contract because of the story nor that he had suffered any financial damage.

Sometimes people decide to sue for malicious falsehood rather than libel because of the costs involved. Legal aid is available for malicious falsehood actions but not for libel.

Pop star Kirk Brandon unsuccessfully sued George O'Dowd (better known as Boy George) for malicious falsehood over claims in O'Dowd's autobiography and a song that the two had had a homosexual relationship in the early 1980s. Brandon admitted in the High Court that the two had shared a bed but denied they had had sex. But Mr Justice Douglas Brown, who had praised Brandon for the way he had handled the case, said he was not satisfied that he had told the truth about his physical relationship with O'Dowd. He was confident that O'Dowd was a truthful witness. The judge said that Brandon's allegations of malice were quite hopeless and should never have been made. Because legal aid was not available for libel the judge claimed the facts had been twisted to fit an allegation of malicious falsehood (news story, *Guardian*, 30 April 1997).

To report that a person has died when he has not cannot result in an action for libel because there is nothing defamatory about death, but it might lead to an action for malicious falsehood. A professional entertainer who earned a living impersonating Al Jolson threatened to sue a newspaper for malicious falsehood after they wrongly reported the entertainer's death.

He said: 'It cost me a fortune in phone calls. You can't just say "I'm alive".' He claimed he had lost work for about six months because of the report. The paper claimed the entertainer's obituary was based on a letter that purported to be from his fan club but which turned out to be a hoax.

Other entertainers have brought malicious falsehood claims. Jazz violinist Stephane Grappelli sued for malicious falsehood after false reports that he was ill and never likely to tour again.

In 1991 actor Gorden Kaye, who featured in the television comedy series *'Allo 'Allo*, threatened to sue the *Sunday Sport* after a reporter from the paper got into Kaye's hospital bedroom and carried out an interview with him although the actor had not completely recovered from an anaesthetic after undergoing brain surgery. The paper intended to publish it as a 'world exclusive' voluntary interview. The Court of Appeal granted an injunction against the newspaper on the grounds that it suggested Kaye appeared to have voluntarily given up what could have been a very lucrative story.

THE LEGAL CONCEPT OF MALICE, OR 'DON'T LET THE FACTS GET IN THE WAY OF A GOOD STORY'

Journalists will lose a claim against them for malicious falsehood if it can be proven that they published untrue statements maliciously. Evidence of malice can also defeat the defences of qualified privilege and fair comment in libel cases.

Malice is present when information is published out of spite or ill-will or from some other dishonest or improper motive or for personal gain or advantage. Journalists are also acting maliciously if they publish statements which they know are untrue, have been told are untrue, or are reckless as to whether they are true or not. But this must be the dominant reason for the publication. It reminds one to beware of the adage: Don't let the facts get in the way of a good story.

Frequent criticism of a company's products is not to be regarded, in itself, as evidence of malice. It could simply be that in the journalist's opinion the company does persistently and consistently produce goods that do not meet the journalist's own standards and expectations. On the other hand, the journalist has to rebut any claims by the plaintiffs that the criticism is part of a well-orchestrated and vindictive campaign against them. This could prove difficult where there is a history of animosity between journalist and complainant.

Regard must be had to the way material is presented. Vigorous, startling banner headlines, typesize out of context with the copy, too prominent a position on the page or in the magazine, strong language, circulation-boosting news-stand advertising are all powerful and persuasive evidence of malice.

A refusal to retract or apologise for offending material or prevarication over such statements also can be claimed as evidence of malice, as can publication of a response that is not agreed in advance and does not meet with the complainant's satisfaction.

CHECKLIST

Before publication:

- Did you carry out tests strictly according to instructions?
- Did you record your findings and check their accuracy?
- Did you set independent witnesses and evidence if necessary?
- Have you discussed with the manufacturer any significant differences between your test results and their claims?
- Are you sure that your presentation of the story does not provide evidence of malice?
- Did you consult your legal adviser when in doubt?
- Have you clarified the qualifications of the reviewer?

After publication:

- Have you responded speedily to any criticism if you were proven to be wrong?
- Did you take immediate steps to check the validity of evidence that supports the article?
- Did you take legal advice before publishing apologies and/or corrections?

Whose copyright is it, anyway?   **8**

INTRODUCTION

Copyright is the basic law of publishing. It is the law that gives authors the right not to have their works unlawfully copied by other people and, conversely, it gives other people the right not to have their works unlawfully copied by anybody else, including journalists.

The important word here is 'unlawfully' because there are instances when journalists can lawfully use other people's copyright material without fear of being sued for infringement, and these are outlined below.

THE PRESENT LAW

In the United Kingdom the most recent law governing copyright is the Copyright Designs and Patents Act 1988 which came into effect on 1 August 1989; but remember that two other pieces of copyright legislation still govern works created between 1911 and 31 July 1989. In theory, therefore, some material will still be protected by those Copyright Acts well into the millennium. This has particular relevance to the reuse of pictures, as is discussed later in this chapter.

International copyright conventions that have been signed by all the major countries in the world and by a great many minor ones too, ensure that journalists in all the signatory nations, of which the UK is one, receive the same protection as do the country's own citizens. So, provided you have complied with UK copyright law, your work will qualify for international copyright recognition. The converse is also true.

Copyright – the right to control copying – exists mainly to protect the fruits of a person's investment of time, labour, skill and judgement in writing stories and features and in the choice and layout of journalistic material. It is known as intellectual property and can be bought and sold, given by will and licensed in a variety of ways. It exists independently of the work it protects, so if you buy a picture you cannot thereby make prints of it.

WORKS THAT ACQUIRE COPYRIGHT

Copyright is concerned with 'works', of which there are three main types:

1   original literary, dramatic, musical and artistic works;
2   sound recordings, films, broadcast or cable programmes;
3   typographical arrangements.

Also included expressly or by definition are computer programs, architectural structures and buildings, databanks, dance and mime, and collages.

The word 'original' does not mean that the work has never been done before but that it must have been originated by a qualified person or a machine. Neither does it have to have any literary merit in the usual sense of the word. A few words scribbled on the back of a holiday postcard attract copyright protection but commonplace words and phrases do not.

Remember, however, that there is no copyright in facts or ideas or in news itself. There is, however, copyright in quotes. This became clear in 1990 when the *Daily Express* and *Today* newspapers sued each other over alleged pirating of copyright in 'exclusive' news stories involving Pamella Bordes, who worked in the Houses of Commons as a researcher, and Marina Ogilvy, an unmarried member of the Royal family.

A Chancery judge said he would hesitate long before deciding there was copyright protection in a news story which another newspaper would infringe if it lifted it and ran it in different words. But the conduct of an interview and the selection of quotations involved at least as much skill and judgement as merely taking down the words of a public speech.

WHO IS PROTECTED?

Since 1 August 1989 the first owner of the copyright in any work, including photographs, is the person who creates it, and the 1988 Act refers to them all as 'authors'. This makes an important change to the ownership of copyright in photographs and commissioned works. Under previous laws the copyright usually belonged to the person who commissioned the work, or, in the case of uncommissioned photographs, to the person who owned the material on which they were taken, and its reuse was never a problem. That is no longer the case.

Simply commissioning words and pictures from freelance journalists without reference to rights now no longer automatically gives editors copyright in them, and freelance contributors need to be aware of this major change so that they can negotiate accordingly. Ownership of copyright must be agreed to be given to editors at the time of the commission which must, according to the 1988 Act, be made in writing otherwise the editors acquire only a licence to use the work once. This is also important when waivers of moral rights are made.

Many magazine companies have introduced standard commissioning letters but this will apply only where there is a company-wide policy. Otherwise editors and freelance contributors must ensure that copyright provisions on all commissioned works, whether words, photographs or other material, are clearly spelled out and understood by both sides. Syndication rights should also be provided for.

Written commissions provide extra protection for freelance journalists and editors because, if they are properly worded, they are also regarded as legally binding contracts so an editor can sue for breach of contract if the material provided by the freelance does not match up to the requirements set out in the commission letter, though this is likely to happen in only the most extreme cases. An alternative is for editors to refuse to pay for material they cannot use because it falls below the standard required, and to decline to give any further commissions to the freelance in question.

Such written commissions also clearly provide protection for freelance contributors when claims for overdue payments are being disputed by editors.

COPYRIGHT IN EMPLOYEES' WORKS

Prior to 1989 the copyright of employees' works depended on their contracts of employment, but since 1989 it belongs to their employers, without exception. This means that journalists who sell their material to other publications – even those not in direct competition – are infringing their employers' copyright and are almost certainly in breach of their employment contracts. This does not mean that journalists cannot write for other publications, but they should do so with their employers' knowledge and consent or the work must be done in their own time.

The author of computer-generated works is afforded copyright protection. The author is the person undertaking the arrangements for the creation of the work. Typographical arrangements are also protected, the author in this case being the publisher of the edition.

THE POSITION OF FREELANCE CONTRIBUTORS

The position of freelance contributors is important in deciding where copyright ownership rests. Freelance journalists, artists and photographers who are employed on 'contracts of service' are regarded as employees even though they might work from home. Copyright in everything they produce – contract apart – belongs to the publishing company by whom they are contracted and should not be sold on by the freelance to other organisations.

Freelance contributors who are employed on 'contracts for services' are not regarded as employees and, as authors, are first owners of the copyright in material they provide. This means that editors must ensure that adequate arrangements are made to protect their ownership of copyright in works submitted by freelance writers, photographers, artists and so on, otherwise they could find it being published elsewhere and, if particularly topical, in advance of their own publication.

REPORTING SPEECHES AND INTERVIEWS

Until the 1988 Act came into effect, people who made speeches and gave interviews did not have their words protected by copyright. Now they do. In such situations, common in journalism, the speaker now owns copyright in his or her words, even if extempore, as soon as a record is made of them whether in a notebook or on a recording because he or she is the author of them.

Can they be reported without fear of infringement? The answer is yes, because the Act permits the use of a record of spoken words for the purpose of reporting current events provided:

1   it is a direct record of the words used;
2   the recording was not prohibited by the speaker;
3   it was not used in a way prohibited by the speaker;
4   the person lawfully in possession of the record authorises its use.

The provision under 2 suggests that in some circumstances speakers could censor the use of their words, and this is true. But any restrictions put on reporting them must be made before the words are spoken, not during or after the event. Even in cases where speakers do impose restrictions reporters can still write news stories or features based on their words because there is no copyright in facts. So, provided the speaker's actual words are not used and there is some checking and re-jigging of the facts, it is believed the courts would hold that there had been no infringement of copyright.

Of course, reporting that Mr X had refused to allow his words to be reported verbatim shows what they are worth! Experience so far indicates that, in cases where speakers have tried to censor reporting of their words, journalists have been able to convince them that to have them accurately reported and made public serves everybody's best interests and stifles rumour, speculation and half-truth.

USING OTHER PEOPLE'S COPYRIGHT MATERIAL

It is common practice, accepted by the courts, for journalists to 'lift' material from other printed sources and use it themselves. In the case referred to above (p. 52), the judge remarked that to rule that such action was a breach of copyright would strike at the root of journalism and lead to the acceptance of a monopoly in a particular piece of news.

This does not mean that journalists can consistently lift stories from other publications and get away with it simply by rewriting them. Wise professional journalists will always check the facts before using them in their own magazines. Even the most experienced journalists get it wrong sometimes and there is no better way of proving that a journalist has lifted somebody else's copy than the repetition of an error, or the use of a story that has come exclusively from one source.

FAIR DEALING

Journalists who want to use other people's words can do so if:

- it is for the purpose of criticism or review, or
- they are reporting current events.

This means that copy written by reporters and feature writers as well as that by critics and reviewers will be protected from actions for infringement when using quotes, provided they do not constitute a substantial part of the text and come within the terms of fairness. In each case there must be a sufficient acknowledgement of the source and the use made must amount to 'fair dealing'.

What constitutes a substantial part in 'fair' dealing is legally undefined and a matter for professional judgement, but anything that would reduce the commercial value to the author in a work would be regarded as use of a substantial part and liable to a claim, for infringement.

By convention, 'fair dealing' is sometimes taken to mean one extract not exceeding 400 words or a total of 800 words in a number of extracts, although in such cases no one extract should be longer than 250 words.

Fair dealing does not apply, however, to news photographs used without permission for reporting current events, so to scan in pictures from another publication would be risky. One best-selling women's magazine is reported to have been paid £7,000 by a national newspaper after it scanned some of the magazine's fashion shots without permission.

Pictures should not be lifted from videos or from television programmes without permission.

Magazines can now publish pictures that incidentally include other artistic works, such as a poster or a picture on the wall in a room setting, without the risk of a claim. It is when journalists try a short cut by using someone else's material as their own that publishers are likely to run into trouble – and rightly so.

WHAT ARE MORAL RIGHTS?

This is the most fundamental change that has been made to copyright law by the 1988 Act. It has already been pointed out that copyright is a form of property, but in continental countries the philosophy is that authors' creations are as much a part of their persona as their physical appearance.

Journalists should be aware of the main principles behind moral rights, though they are not likely to be a problem because of the exceptions written into the UK law.

Authors of copyright works have the right to be identified as such. They also have the right not to have their work subjected to derogatory treatment: this means that changes which in any way reflect on an author's honour or reputation or that amount to distortion or mutilation of a work, as, for example, including a landscape artist's drawing in a pornographic display or reproducing it with poor colour registration, would be classed as derogatory treatment.

The practical day-to-day implications of the introduction of moral rights into magazine journalism were horrendous. It would have meant that every writer of even the shortest paragraph would have been entitled to a by-line; sub-editors would not have been able to alter copy without the author's permission nor crop photographs without consulting the photographer for fear of breaching their moral rights. It simply would not have worked. Fortunately the publishing industry lobby was sufficiently persuasive during the Copyright Bill's progress through Parliament to convince the government that changes were necessary.

Consequently there are exceptions to an author's moral rights. They do not attach to

1   an employee's work;
2   computer-generated works;
3   any work made for the purpose of publication in newspapers, magazines or similar periodicals or in an encyclopedia, dictionary, yearbook or other collective work of reference;
4   any work made available with the consent of the author for the purposes of such publication, i.e. under 3;
5   any work made for the purpose of reporting current events.

The exception under 3 covers freelance material and 4 covers any material that comes into a journalist's possession that was not intended for publication (such as written reports) but where the author has given consent to its use – provided, of course, that the author is not an employee, in which case ownership of copyright would belong to the employer.

WHEN AN AUTHOR IS NOT AN AUTHOR

Although the 1988 Act gives authors the right to be identified as such, both the 1956 and the 1988 Acts also give them the right not to have work falsely attributed to them.

The editor of a weekly football magazine commissioned a freelance artist to produce a drawing showing how a goal had been scored at a Saturday match. Included in the drawing was a first-person account by the footballer of how he had shot the ball into the net. He subsequently threatened to sue the magazine for false attribution because he had not been interviewed and the words had obviously been made up. The magazine reportedly paid him £400 – his normal fee for an interview.

When a regular contributor to a magazine failed to get his copy in on time the editor wrote the column but put the contributor's by-line on it. The contributor threatened to sue for false attribution. It might be that he could also have sued the magazine for libel if he believed the journalism had an adverse effect on his professional integrity or reputation by, for example, expressing opinions which were known to be contrary to his own.

In 1972 the singer Dorothy Squires, at one time married to actor Roger Moore, successfully sued a newspaper for false attribution of authorship in an interview with her in which, she claimed, some of the quotes had been made up.

More recently, in 1988 an expert nutritionist who had been commissioned to write a feature for a daily newspaper successfully sued when he found his by-line on another feature he had not written and which put forward opinions with which he strongly disagreed.

A RIGHT TO PRIVACY

There is no general right to privacy in Britain, but now people who commission photographs for private and domestic purposes, that is family album type pictures, can sue if those pictures are published without their permission.

Imagine that a mother commissions photographs of her son who has just been awarded a private pilot's licence. Some months later he is killed in a flying accident. The commercial photographer sees the value in such a picture and offers it to a magazine or other publication for a fat fee. The mother will not own the copyright – unless she acquired it at the time of the commission, which is unlikely – but she does own privacy rights and controls the photograph's circulation and distribution and could sue for breach of her privacy rights.

Beware, therefore, when using this kind of picture in human-interest features when they are supplied by somebody else. This change in the law was necessary because, prior to the 1988 Act, commissioning a photograph usually vested copyright in the commissioner and the photographer would not have been in a position to offer it for sale.

ACQUIRING RIGHTS AND LICENCES

Publishing material produced other than by employees must be done by acquiring either rights or licences.

'All Rights' entitle magazines to exclusive use of the material anywhere in the world, at any time and in any form. The author is barred from selling on the material but the magazine can permit its use, either for a fee or free of charge. Editors and freelance writers and photographers must calculate value for use before buying or selling material on an All Rights basis.

Rights other than All Rights can be acquired in terms of time, territory, language or form. Editors and freelance contributors can negotiate partial rights to publish material before or after a certain date, in a specified country or countries in specified languages and in a particular form – for example, in a magazine.

For an editor, it is wise to acquire rights to cover a whole range of magazines rather than just one. The fact that a company with scores of titles commissions material for a particular magazine does not mean that that same material can be used automatically in any of the company's other publications.

All commissions for work should be in writing and must spell out the rights being assigned. One copy of the commission letter must be signed by the person selling the rights.

First Rights, often referred to as First Use, give the publisher the right to be the first to use the material anywhere in the world. After it has been published it cannot be re-used without the copyright owner's permission. First EU rights, previously known as first British Serial Rights, as the name implies give publishers the right to be the first to use the material in EU countries. Such rights are known as exclusive licences and must be in writing and signed by the copyright owner.

Unsolicited material such as press releases and readers' letters is publishable under non-exclusive licences. Copyright owners can consent to publication of their works without any fee or assignment of rights.

MAKE A NOTE OF IT

Material, particularly photographs, should be dated and some record kept of the rights that have been assigned, unless the publisher has acquired All Rights. Constant re-use of a photograph in which the publisher had acquired only First Use is reported to have cost one company £15,000 in damages. Introduce a system to ensure that such mistakes cannot happen.

HOW LONG DOES COPYRIGHT LAST?

The general principle is that copyright lasts during the life of the author and for seventy years after his or her death. Photographs are no longer an exception and have a similar copyright life. Computer-generated works are in copyright for fifty years from the end of the calendar year in which they were made. Typographical arrangements of a published edition remain in copyright for twenty-five years from the year in which that typographical arrangement was first published, provided it is not a copy of a previous typographical arrange-ment. So be particularly careful when using illustrations of typographical layouts from other publications – often referred to as 'ragouts'. Copyright in databases depends upon whether the contents are original literacy works or not. If they are not, protection lasts fifteen years, but this period is rolled on if the database is updated.

IN THE PUBLIC INTEREST

Journalists who are sued for infringement of copyright now have a defence of public interest, though this is unlikely to apply in any but the most serious of cases.

In 1984 legal action by a company meant that the *Daily Express* was faced with an injunction restraining publication of information about a new product. The newspaper successfully argued that it was in the public interest to report that the document showed a new type of breathalyser was unreliable and could result in motorists being wrongly convicted of drink-driving offences. The newspaper had obtained the information in a 'leaked' memo from company employees, copyright in which belonged not to the employees but to the company. This case is discussed in more detail in Chapter 10.

PENALTIES FOR INFRINGEMENT

Journalists can be sued either for infringement of copyright in a civil law case or be prosecuted as criminals. Civil proceedings could result in imposition of damages, an injunction to prevent further breaches, and an order to hand over any remaining copies. In criminal proceedings journalists could be subject to a fine and/or imprisonment.

CHECKLIST

Before publication:

- Have you checked the copyright position of unsolicited material unless it is routine text such as a press release; reader's letter and so on? Some public relations firms have sent out photographs for which they had not acquired the right to authorise publication, and editors have had to pick up the bill.
- Did you make sure that the commission letter not only sets out details of the material required but also settles the question of copyright assignment, and get signed acceptance?
- Did you follow up verbal commissions with a letter where necessary?
- Have you given sufficient acknowledgement to copy gleaned from other publications?
- Did you check that family album type pictures, either from a commercial photographer or a close family member, do not infringe anyone's privacy rights?

After publication:

- Have you made a formal record of rights acquired in words and pictures, unless you have a consistent policy?
- If you have different rights for different journalistic material, have you made sure a record is kept for individual pieces to avoid wrongful re-use?
- If commissioned material did not meet the standards required, or could not be used at all, have you considered whether it is worth taking any action when settling the bill?

Don't be held in contempt   9

INTRODUCTION

Journalists writing for and working on magazines are far less likely than newspaper journalists to be involved in questions of contempt of court, because magazines carry fewer crime and court stories and it is from these that most contempt actions arise.

Nevertheless, it is important that they are aware of the danger areas and the main provisions of the Contempt of Court Act 1981 so that they can avoid the often severe punitive consequences of getting it wrong. A summary of the main provisions of the Act is given below and a more detailed account at the end of this chapter.

THE RIGHT TO A FAIR TRIAL

Common and statutory contempt laws exist to protect the right to a fair trial of people in civil and criminal court proceedings and the due administration of the judicial system. The basic principle of justice is that everyone is entitled to be regarded as innocent until proven guilty (or liable in civil proceedings) and that that is a job for the courts, not the media.

Publication of anything that prejudices or interferes with that right can be regarded as a contempt of court. It is important, therefore, when journalists are writing or sub-editing copy involving a crime or civil law matter or a court case, to know exactly how far they can go.

A SIMPLE TEST

The simple test is: Could this statement prejudge the result of court proceedings? If it could, then it should not appear in print.

For example, to report that a man had committed a crime rather than that he had been accused of doing so would be a contempt of court (and also defamatory if he was not charged with the offence or was acquitted). To say that a company was not responsible for injuries suffered by an employee who is suing them could be contempt of the civil court proceedings. Commenting on a trial while it is in progress can in some circumstances be held a contempt of court, though reporting the trial within the terms of the 1981 Act is not.

Dr Leonard Arthur, a paediatrician, appeared at Leicester Crown Court accused of murdering a three-day-old mongoloid baby boy by giving instructions that he should be treated with a drug which had caused him to die from starvation. While the trial was running, a *Sunday Express* columnist referred to the case and said the baby had been drugged instead of being fed and had died 'unloved, unwanted'. The columnist was subsequently prosecuted for contempt of court and fined £1,000. Lord Justice Watkins said the article could not be regarded as anything but a scathing reference to the trial and the person on trial. It was of the utmost importance that 'extraneous, irrelevant and emotional influences should not enter the minds of the jurors.'

Similarly, the High Court first held that the *Daily Mail* had been in contempt of court by publishing on the third day of the same trial an article about the sanctity of life in support of a Pro-life candidate at a by-election. The publishers were fined £500 and ordered to pay the Attorney General's legal costs. The editor and publishers appealed to the House of Lords, where Lord Diplock commented that it was clear that the article, written by Malcolm Muggeridge, was capable of prejudicing the jury against the paediatrician and that at that stage of the trial the risk was substantial and not remote. The fact that the paediatrician was subsequently acquitted was immaterial.

DISCUSSION OF PUBLIC AFFAIRS

But the Law Lords said the article also fell within sec. 5 of the Contempt of Court Act 1981, being published in good faith as a discussion of public affairs. Lord Diplock pointed out that there was no mention of the trial in the article. It might be that jurors would think: 'That is the sort of thing Dr Arthur is being tried for; it appears to be something that quite a lot of doctors do.' But the risk of them thinking that and allowing it to prejudice their minds against the paediatrician was 'merely incidental'.

In 1984 the trial by jury at Reading Crown Court of twelve women from the peace camp at Greenham Common, Newbury, Berkshire, had to be abandoned because a feature in the *Daily Express* while the trial was in progress had named one of the defendants. They had been accused of criminal damage at the nearby cruise missile base. The judge told the jury: 'We don't have in this country verdict by newspaper, we have verdict by jury.'

In March 1997 Sir Nicholas Lyell, the Attorney General, instituted contempt of court proceedings against the *Evening Standard* after the newspaper published an article that caused a trial to be abandoned. The newspaper's editor, Max Hastings, had unreservedly apologised to the trial judge.

Previously the Attorney General had told the House of Commons in answer to a parliamentary question that at least five criminal cases had been stopped in three years because judges had decided that media coverage would make a fair trial impossible.

Headlines such as MEDIA COVERAGE STOPS TRIALS, JUDGE BLAMES MEDIA AS HE HALTS ASSAULT TRIAL, APPEAL COURT ORDERS BOMB PLOT RETRIAL are not uncommon.

THERE ARE EXCEPTIONS

But the Attorney General was unsuccessful when he prosecuted five national newspapers over the trial of Geoffrey Knights, boyfriend of Gillian Taylforth, an actress in the BBC soap *Eastenders*. Knights had been accused of wounding a taxi driver but the trial was stopped after the judge referred to 'unlawful, misleading and scandalous' pre-trial media publicity.

Judges in the High Court decided that the contempt allegations should be dismissed, having due regard to the extensive coverage of the relationship between the actress and Mr Knights and the already public knowledge that Mr Knights had previous convictions.

Journalists who are asked by the police for help in tracking down people wanted for questioning will not normally be in contempt of court, even though a warrant has been issued for that person's arrest.

The 1981 Act also provides journalists with a defence of innocent publication where they have taken reasonable care.

REPORTING COURT PROCEEDINGS

Reporting court proceedings is not a contempt of court if handled in good faith but sometimes lawyers take exception to the way in which some newspapers report trials.

In 1995 the *Taylor Sisters* case made news when they complained about the way in which four national newspapers had reported their trial on charges of murder. Michelle and Lisa Taylor initially complained that media coverage was prejudicial and sensationalised but the House of Lords upheld a decision by the High Court that the Solicitor General, acting on behalf of the Attorney General, was entitled not to take action against the newspapers.

Similar allegations were made about the way in which the trial of Rosemary West, convicted of ten murders, was also reported by some sections of the media.

Journalists also can be held to be in contempt of court by any conduct that is likely to bring justice into disrepute or to scandalise it. It is one thing to criticise a judge over a particular sentence he has passed; it is quite another to question his integrity or impartiality.

The Act also imposes a ban on interviewing jurors and on tape recording court proceedings. Courts also have the power to suppress publication of names and the whole or parts of legal proceedings.

Sec. 10 of the Act is intended to provide protection for journalists who are required to reveal their sources, and this is dealt with in more detail in Chapter 10.

AN OUTLINE GUIDE TO THE CONTEMPT OF COURT ACT 1981

SECTION 1

This explains 'the strict liability rule' as that rule of law which treats publication of some information as contempt of court regardless of intent to interfere with the course of justice.

SECTION 2(2)

The rule applies only to a publication which creates a substantial risk that the course of justice in the proceedings in question will be seriously impeded or prejudiced.

SECTION 2(3 & 4): TIME OF LIABILITY FOR CONTEMPT IN CIVIL PROCEEDINGS

Proceedings are deemed to be active for contempt purposes where the case is set down for trial, or when a date is fixed for the case to be heard. Check with the solicitors for either side or the Clerk of the Lists at the court. Liability ceases when the case is disposed of or proceedings are discontinued or withdrawn.

When the risk of contempt starts in criminal proceedings

Criminal proceedings are *active* when:

- an arrest has been made without warrant;
- a warrant has been issued for arrest;
- a summons has been issued or an indictment served;
- an oral charge has been made

Police appeals for public assistance

If a warrant has been issued for a person's arrest and the police ask the press to help in finding that person it is unlikely that the press shall be guilty of contempt even though the proceedings are active. Care should be taken, however, to ensure that background material is not included.

The Attorney-General said in the House of Commons during the debate on the Bill:

> It is plainly right that the police should be able to warn the public through the Press that a particular suspect is dangerous and should not be tackled, or it may simply be that they issue a photograph or some other identification of the wanted man . . . the Press has nothing whatever to fear from publishing *in reasoned terms* anything which may assist in the apprehension of a wanted man and I hope that it will continue to perform this public service.

Appeals and liability for contempt

Appellate proceedings are active from the time when they are commenced, either by application for leave to appeal or application for review, or even by notice of such an application. Liability for contempt, therefore, resumes at any one of these times and ends again after the appeal has been heard, unless a new trial is ordered or the case remitted to a lower court.

When the contempt risk ends

In criminal proceedings the risk ceases to apply if:

- the arrested person is released without being charged;
- no arrest is made within twelve months of the issue of a warrant;
- the case is discontinued;
- the defendant is acquitted or sentenced;
- the defendant is found unfit to be tried, or unfit to plead, or the court orders the charge to lie on file.

Under the fourth point above, therefore, it is possible for the journalist and his or her publication still to be liable for contempt even though a jury has returned a guilty verdict and the defendant is merely awaiting sentence by the judge.

Care must be taken not to report matter arising out of one trial that is likely to be prejudicial to other criminal proceedings.

SECTION 3: DEFENCE OF INNOCENT PUBLICATION

The Act provides a defence of 'innocent publication' and there is no contempt if, *having taken all reasonable care*, the publication did not know and had no reason to suspect that proceedings were 'active'. If a person is at the police station involuntarily, he is deemed to be under arrest, whether or not the proper arrest procedures have taken place. In some cases where the police have other suspects in mind, they may not wish to disclose that they have arrested one person. Often, the Press will not know that a warrant for arrest has been issued. This means that care must be taken to record the details of enquiries made, the time and the police contact.

Burden of proof on the reporter

However, the burden of proof in establishing that all reasonable care was taken is upon the journalist accused of contempt.

SECTION 4: REPORTING COURT PROCEEDINGS

A person is not guilty of contempt of court under the strict liability rule in respect of a fair and accurate report of legal proceedings held in public, published contemporaneously *and in good faith*. This is, therefore, unlike the absolute protection given to publications in respect of fair and accurate contemporaneous reports of court proceedings under the defamation laws.

Court reporting and contempt

The Act gives the courts power to rule that some matters should not be reported for the time being:

> The court may, where it appears to be necessary for avoiding the substantial risk of serious prejudice to the administration of justice in those proceedings, or in any other proceedings, pending or imminent, order that the publication of any report of those proceedings or any part of those proceedings be postponed for such period as the court thinks necessary for that purpose.

SECTION 5: DISCUSSION OF PUBLIC AFFAIRS

Part of the government's response to the European Court's ruling on the *Sunday Times* thalidomide case was to introduce a new defence against a charge of contempt. The Act says that a publication made as, or as part of, a discussion in good faith of public affairs is not to be treated as contempt of court under the strict liability rule if the risk of impediment or prejudice to particular legal proceedings is merely incidental to the discussion.

SECTION 6: OTHER CONDUCT

Liability is not restricted to conduct creating a substantial risk of serious prejudice; any other conduct may still be a contempt if it is intended to create prejudice.

SECTION 7: PROCEEDINGS FOR CONTEMPT

Proceedings for contempt under the strict liability rule can be taken by a crown court or by a higher court, or by the Attorney-General or by some other person with his consent.

SECTION 8: INTERVIEWING JURORS

It is contempt of court to seek or disclose information about the deliberations of voting in the jury room.

Mr David Pallister, a *Guardian* reporter, was alleged to be in contempt of court after a woman juror said he had spoken to her during the lunch break of a smuggling trial, even though the jury had given their verdicts.

SECTION 9: TAPE RECORDINGS

It is contempt of court under the Act to use, or take into court to use, any tape recorder (except by permission of the court) or to make any recording.

SECTION 10: JOURNALISTS' SOURCES

No court may require a person to disclose, nor is any person guilty of contempt of court for refusing to disclose, the source of information contained in a publication for which he is responsible, *unless it is established to the satisfaction of the court that disclosure is necessary in the interests of justice or national security, or for the prevention of disorder or crime.*

This widens the discretion of judges to refuse to order journalists to reveal their sources in some cases, but there may still be many cases where journalists will have no special protection. Judges have great latitude in deciding when disclosure is necessary, as the case against William Goodwin, reported on p. 75, illustrates.

SECTION 11: POWER TO SUPPRESS PUBLICATION OF NAMES

The courts have power, when they withhold a name from being mentioned in public in their proceedings, to direct that the name or other matter should not be published. This power is intended to tighten up the law to prevent blackmail victims and people involved in national security and secret processes from being identified.

This restriction does not affect those imposed on court proceedings under other legislation, such as reports of remands and committals, rape cases and so on; these restrictions must still be observed.

SECTION 12: MAGISTRATES COURTS

Magistrates can jail or impose a fine of up to £2,500 for anyone insulting them, any witness, lawyer or officer of the court, or who interrupts the proceedings or misbehaves. They cannot act directly against contempt by publication but may refer the matter to the Attorney-General.

SECTION 14: PENALTIES FOR CONTEMPT

Penalties can be imprisonment and/or fine.

SECTION 20: CONTEMPT AND TRIBUNALS

The Act defines 'court' as 'any tribunal exercising the judicial power of the State', and this probably means industrial tribunals; it also applies to any tribunal to which the Tribunals of Inquiry (Evidence) Act 1921 applies. In such cases the contempt risk begins from the *time the tribunal is appointed* until its report is presented to Parliament.

CHECKLIST

- Is the contempt risk 'active' within the terms of the Contempt of Court Act 1981?
- Does court copy contain any reference to other legal proceedings pending or imminent?
- Do court reports meet the test of 'good faith'?
- Can publication of background features be defended as a discussion of public affairs?
- Is anything being published that has been suppressed by the court?
- Has legal advice been taken, if appropriate?

Strictly confidential

10

INTRODUCTION

Problems of confidentiality are difficult for journalists because, on the one hand, they are often in the possession of sensitive information which they believe their readers have a right to know, and yet, on the other hand, they can feel restrained from publishing it because they are in danger of revealing sources they feel obliged to protect.

WHAT MAKES INFORMATION 'CONFIDENTIAL'?

Not every communication that has 'in confidence' attached to it will be protected by an action for breach of confidence. To be protected the information must have been received in a relationship of confidence, for example between husband and wife or in employment or by contract.

Additionally, it could be that the circumstances of communication themselves call for the recipient to be prevented from taking unfair advantage of it. Typical examples would be disclosing an invention to a prospective manufacturer with a view to persuading him or her to take it up, or making personal gain from the use of market-sensitive information.

Journalists who come into possession of confidential information need to make enquiries into its content, verify its accuracy and speak to people who might be involved. By doing so, of course, they alert these people to the fact that the confidential material has been divulged and risk the granting by the courts of injunctions restraining publication.

In such cases it is wise to approach other non-confidential sources to carry out checks on its accuracy. If an injunction is granted, then the documents containing the confidential information will become court property and to destroy or mutilate them at this stage to avoid identification of a source would be treated as a contempt of court.

However, you cannot be ordered to hand over to the court any documents that you have destroyed after the information has been published but before you receive a court order to do so, though the courts will take a critical view of such deliberate action.

Publishing confidential material before asking questions about its accuracy runs the risk of the journalist being sued for libel if it turns out to be false. There is a particular danger with 'leaked' information or any 'unlawfully obtained' because the general principle is that there is no privilege attached to it.

Britain has no statutory law of confidence and the action has developed as a matter of equity: that is, as an attempt by the courts to provide remedies where common law rules were too harsh or relief was not available.

Historically it was a lawsuit favoured by industrialists, who used it to protect secret processes; but over the past forty years or so it has become increasingly used by individuals, companies and organisations who wish to stop confidential and 'private' personal information getting into the public domain – especially through the media – or to rivals.

PROTECTED MATERIAL

Actions for breach of confidence are used to protect a wide range of material from exposure, including copyright works, trade and industrial secrets, technical specifications, commercially sensitive information and stories relating to personal and moral behaviour.

THE NATURE OF CONFIDENTIAL MATERIAL

In a case in 1969 Mr Justice Megarry outlined the formula for successful actions for breach of confidence and delineated three requirements:

1   the information must have the necessary quality of confidence about it. Usually it will relate to commercial and/or industrial matters but can include issues of personal morality such as sexual behaviour, discussions between husband and wife and other private relationships;
2   it must have been given in circumstances importing an obligation of confidence, for example by terms of employment or contract specifically providing for such confidence; and
3   the use of such information must have been unauthorised.

INFORMATION IN THE PUBLIC DOMAIN

Once the confidential information has been published or communicated to a third party it falls into the public domain and breach of confidence actions will not prevent its subsequent publication.

Journalists receiving such information who did not know of its confidential nature or could not reasonably have been aware of it can publish it. Any consequential action for breach of confidence would, then, be taken against the person passing the information to the journalist but not against the journalist.

In the *Spycatcher* case involving a former government employee, Peter Wright, in 1988, the House of Lords refused to grant an injunction preventing the *Observer* and the *Guardian* newspapers from publishing extracts from Wright's book because its contents had been widely published overseas, thus failing Mr Justice Megarry's first test.

THE DISTINCTION BETWEEN BREACH OF CONFIDENCE AND PRIVACY

Although breach of confidence and privacy are commonly thought to be one and the same, they are not. In its report on breach of confidence in 1981 the Law Commission took great care to set out the distinction by stating that the term 'breach of confidence' related to 'the disclosure or use (i) of information in breach of confidence and (ii) of information "unlawfully obtained"', and it is based on an obligation of confidence owed by one person to another:

> By contrast, a right of privacy in respect of information would arise from the nature of the information itself: it would be based on the principle that certain kinds of information are categorised as private and for that reason alone ought not to be disclosed.

As far as is possible the Law Commission's distinction is followed in this book and a more detailed discussion of privacy is included in Chapter 11.

CONFIDENCE BETWEEN EMPLOYER AND EMPLOYEE

The only people who can sue for breach of confidence are the individuals or organisations who imparted the original information in confidence.

Companies can take action where breach of confidence is by an employee because all employees owe a duty of confidence to their employers. This policy is designed to prevent employees from passing on 'trade secrets' to others while in that company's employment although the courts would take a different attitude if the information was about criminal activities or where divulging the information was in the public interest.

The situation is rather different for ex-employees whose duty of confidence ends when their employment ends unless their terms of employment continue to forbid disclosure. Common examples are servants of the Royal Family, prominent sports people and the staff of entertainers.

THE POSITION OF JOURNALISTS

If an employee passes on information about his or her employer in confidence to a journalist, the employer will not be able to sue the journalist for breach of confidence if that information is subsequently published because there is no contractual obligation between the employer and the journalist, only between employer and employee. The employer would have to obtain an injunction restraining publication on the grounds of a contractual breach of confidence by the employee. The employer could obtain an injunction prior to publication if the journalist knows or ought to have known the confidential nature of the material (see *X* v *Y*, pp. 72–3).

Publication could, however, lead to an action for libel or malicious falsehood against the journalist if the information is defamatory or false and financially damaging and possibly to an action for infringement of copyright.

IN THE PUBLIC INTEREST, OR JUST INTERESTING TO THE PUBLIC?

In 1984 the *Daily Express* obtained information in confidence from employees of Lion Laboratories that they had doubts about the reliability of a new breathalyser – the Lion Intoximeter 3,000 – which had been used to test motorists suspected of drink-driving. The company obtained an injunction restraining publication of the information because it was confidential and claimed that publication would also be in breach of the company's copyright.

The *Daily Express* appealed, and the appeal was allowed on the grounds that a defence of public interest applied to the issues of confidence and copyright because the public interest in that case was best served by the information being published and the plaintiffs would be left to their remedy in damages.

The Court of Appeal said that many people had been prosecuted on the basis of the Intoximeter test and that its accuracy was a matter of grave concern. It added that, although it would be inappropriate for the Press to carry out a technical reappraisal of the equipment, it was a very important, even essential, function of the Press to campaign to put pressure on the authorities to take notice.

Lord Justice Griffiths said: 'We would all be the worse off if the Press were unduly inhibited in this field of activity.' The judge also pointed out 'where the Press raise the defence of public interest, the court must appraise it critically'. The court pointed out that there was a difference between what was in the public interest and what was simply interesting to the public.

In *Francome* v *Daily Mirror Group Newspapers*, illegally taped private telephone conversations disclosed a breach of Jockey Club Rules and possibly a criminal conspiracy. The court granted an injunction to restrain publication, taking the view that 'in the instant case, pending trial, it is impossible to see what public interest could be served by publishing the contents of these tapes which would not equally be served by giving them to the police or to the Jockey Club. Any wider publication could only serve the interests of the *Daily Mirror*.'

In 1987 in a High Court case referred to as *X* v *Y*, it was revealed that an employee of a health authority had passed information to a newspaper that two doctors were being allowed to continue practising even though they were receiving treatment for Aids. The court issued an injunction preventing the newspaper from publishing a story which would have identified the two doctors and the hospital where they were being treated, based on information obtained through a breach of confidence by a health authority employee.

Mr Justice Rose said that the public interest in maintaining the confidentiality of patients' hospital records far outweighed the public interest in freedom of the Press. He claimed that allowing publication would enable the newspaper to procure breaches of confidence and then select what was to be published. That would make a mockery of the law's protection of confidentiality when no justifying public interest had been shown.

Barclays Bank suspended three of its employees in January 1996 while it investigated allegations that they had leaked the name of a National Lottery winner to the *Sun* after seeing the winning cheque being processed. The winner had told Camelot, the lottery organisers, that he did not want publicity. Later an MP said such breaches of confidence should be made a criminal offence.

PROTECTION OF SOURCES

Journalists have always maintained that respecting the wishes of contacts not to be identified under any circumstances is a matter of conscience and professional and ethical practice.

If they were perceived by the public to be lacking in moral fibre and integrity by their willingness to reveal their sources, the supply of valuable information would dry up and the public interest would suffer. Relying on informants to pass on newsworthy information in confidence is sometimes the only way journalists can operate.

Indeed, both the Press Complaints Commission (PCC) Code of Practice and the Code of Conduct of the National Union of Journalists (NUJ) have clauses stressing the need for confidentiality of sources. The PCC says: 'Journalists have a moral obligation to protect sources of information.' Although the NUJ code does not make specific reference to a moral obligation by journalists, it does require them to give similar protection to confidential sources of information.

'OFF THE RECORD . . .'

Informants who want to pass on information to journalists 'off the record' should be regarded with caution. Wise journalists will first ask themselves: Why are they telling me this? What's in it for them? Do they have an axe to grind?

Once you have made a promise to receive information 'off the record' you should abide by it, but let your informant know that you must feel free to pursue your enquiries from other, preferably attributable, sources and that any subsequent publication of the information should not be regarded as a deliberate breach of confidence.

CONTEMPT OF COURT

Until 1981 journalists had no statutory protection against an order by a judge to reveal a source and they were liable to a fine or a term of imprisonment or both if they disobeyed the judge's order because it was regarded as a contempt of court.

In the *Vassall Spy Tribunal* case in 1963, two journalists went to prison after refusing to name the sources on which they were able to base stories regarding Vassall's private life. The journalists had no statutory defence and they could not persuade their informants to release them from their duty of confidence.

It was not until almost twenty years later that Parliament gave some protection to journalists who were ordered by the courts to reveal their sources and had refused. The Contempt of Court Act 1981, Sec. 10 provides:

No court may require a person to disclose, nor is any person guilty of contempt of court for refusing to disclose, the source of information contained in a publication for which he [*sic*] is responsible, unless it is established to the satisfaction of the court that disclosure is necessary in the interests of justice or national security, or for the prevention of disorder or crime.

In 1983 the *Guardian* published details of a confidential memorandum prepared by the then Secretary of State for Defence, Michael Heseltine, involving the arrival in Britain of cruise missiles, and leaked to them anonymously by a civil servant, Sarah Tisdall. The government demanded that the newspaper return the document and the newspaper initially refused using Sec. 10 in its defence.

The issue was eventually heard by the Law Lords, who ruled that the protection of national security was paramount; the document was handed back, revealing Ms Tisdall as the source. She was subsequently prosecuted under the Official Secrets Act and went to prison for six months.

Had the newspaper destroyed the document before the legal proceedings had begun, the confidentiality of its source would have been preserved, but to destroy the document after the proceedings had started would itself have been a contempt of court.

Jeremy Warner, a reporter on the *Independent* in 1988 published information received in confidence regarding allegations of insider dealing in the City and was subsequently ordered by a government inspector to reveal his source; this was held to be necessary in the interests of preventing crime. The journalist refused and was fined £20,000 and ordered to pay legal costs in the case.

Similarly a trainee journalist called William Goodwin, who worked on the *Engineer* magazine, received confidential information alleging that a company was in financial difficulties and was seeking financial support to keep it afloat. He approached the company for comment but they sought, and were granted, an injunction preventing publication on the grounds of breach of confidence and persuaded the judge to order Goodwin to reveal his source. He refused and was prosecuted for contempt of court, but his claim of a defence under Sec. 10 of the Contempt of Court Act was denied and he was fined £5,000.

The case went on appeal to the House of Lords but it was refused. Lord Bridge said that journalists could not be left to decide for themselves what was necessary for disclosure and what was not. In the meantime it was estimated that legal costs amounted to £250,000.

Subsequently, the case was heard by the European Court of Human Rights, which ruled in favour of the journalist and awarded him £37,500 in legal costs and expenses.

Granada Television in 1980 received confidential documents from a 'mole' at the British Steel Corporation which were highly critical of the way in which the Corporation was being managed. The television company wanted to use them as part of a current affairs programme but the court ordered their return to BSC. Granada refused to name the source but, when threatened with proceedings for contempt, the 'mole' identified himself.

Conversely, the courts will sometimes refuse to order journalists to reveal their sources. In the case involving the leak of confidential information by a health authority employee (see pp. 72–3) the authority wanted to know the source of the information. The issue was whether ordering the journalist to reveal his sources was necessary 'in the interests of justice'.

Explaining his decision not to order identification, Mr Justice Rose said that the term 'justice', the interests of which are entitled to protection, is not used in a general sense as the antonym of 'injustice' but in the technical sense of the administration of justice in the course of legal proceedings in a court of law. He declared that in the present case the identity of the source was not necessary to support the claim for an injunction and disclosure was not necessary 'in the interests of justice'.

STATUTORY REQUIREMENTS FOR DISCLOSURE

In addition to orders under the Contempt of Court Act 1981, some other legislation also requires journalists to reveal their sources when ordered to do so.

The Official Secrets Act 1920 states in Sec. 6 that where a chief officer of police is satisfied that there is reasonable ground for believing that an offence under Official Secrets legislation has been committed, he can ask the Home Secretary to authorise a senior police officer to require a person to reveal the relevant information or in exceptional circumstances can order disclosure without first obtaining the Home Secretary's permission. A journalist who fails to comply with this request commits an offence.

Under Sec. 8 of the Police and Criminal Evidence Act 1984, a Justice of the Peace can issue a search warrant for any material on premises that is likely to be of substantial value in a criminal investigation, although excluded and special procedure material is exempt. Excluded material includes personal, business or professional records held in confidence and 'journalistic material' such as documents or records acquired and created and held under an obligation of confidence. Special procedure material includes business or professional records but not personal records held under a duty of confidence and journalistic material other than excluded material.

Some material will be protected by legal privilege and this would include documents and information connected with legal proceedings.

Proposed changes in the data protection legislation may substantially change the law in this area.

CHECKLIST

Before publication:

- Does the material meet 'the nature of confidence' test?
- Is it in the public domain?
- Have you verified its accuracy?
- Do you have evidence that it is true?
- Is it defamatory or otherwise potentially damaging financially if false?
- Would a 'public interest' defence be sustainable?
- Can you defend an order to reveal your sources under the requirements of Sec. 10 of the Contempt of Court Act 1981?

After publication:

- Did you respond to any complaint promptly without admitting liability?
- Did you collect together all the relevant evidence and discuss possible further action with your legal adviser?

The public's interest in privacy 11

INTRODUCTION

If there were a workable, faultproof definition of privacy it would no doubt by now have been enshrined in statute and the discussion in this chapter would have taken a different course.

Despite an impressive history over the past forty years of private members' bills, committees, Royal Commissions and consultative documents, the fact remains that in the UK what is widely accepted as everybody's inherent right to enjoy a private lifestyle free from gratuitous and unwarranted intrusion and publicity cannot be enforced as a legal right.

Indeed, a consultation paper on infringement of privacy issued by the Lord Chancellor's Department in July 1993 questions whether such a definition is possible or necessary. It claims:

> The question does not require a watertight statutory definition to be settled from the beginning. What is needed is an understanding of 'privacy', in ordinary speech, before legal definitions are brought into play. Privacy is not only the concern of Parliament and lawyers, but of psychologists, sociologists, political scientists and indeed of every individual.

The government's response to the House of Commons National Heritage Select Committee on privacy and media intrusion, published in July 1995, suggests that if legislation were to be introduced then a right to privacy would include:

- a right to be free from harassment and molestation; and
- a right to privacy of personal information, communications and documents.

Personal information would cover, in particular, details about health and medical treatment; marriage, family life and personal relationships; sexual orientation and behaviour; political and religious beliefs; and personal legal and financial affairs.

Such a broadly based approach would mean that much of what appears in print today would be forbidden or actionable under a proposed new civil law tort with a remedy in damages, injunction, account of profits and order to deliver up all documents in the publishing company's possession.

A committee chaired by Sir David Calcutt QC recommended the introduction of criminal offences of entering or remaining on private property without the occupant's consent and would have outlawed the use of surveillance devices, taking photographs, or recording the voices, of individuals on private property without their consent and with a view to publication.

THE PRESS COMPLAINTS COMMISSION CODE

Among the publishing industry's codes of practice regarding privacy, that of the Press Complaints Commission (PCC) is the most specific and the only one under which the public can take any action. (It is reproduced as Appendix 4 to this book.)

Clause 4 of the Code of Practice states:

Intrusions and enquiries into an individual's private life without his or her consent, including the use of long-lens photography to take pictures of people on private property without their consent, are not generally acceptable and publication can only be justified when in the public interest.

The public interest is defined as: detecting or exposing crime or a serious misdemeanour; protecting public health and safety; and preventing the public from being misled by some statement or action of an individual or organisation. Proof of publication in the public interest for any other reasons will be the responsibility of editors.

LEGISLATION VERSUS SELF-REGULATION

At the time of writing none of the recommendations has been put into effect because Parliament and the publishing industry agree that self-regulation is the preferred option.

The then National Heritage Secretary, Virginia Bottomley, in a letter to Lord Wakeham, chairman of the Press Complaints Commission, which was published in the Select Committee report mentioned above, wrote:

We share the aim of preserving the freedom of the press, and at the same time ensuring proper ways of acting against press abuses and providing redress where they do occur ... in this way we shall move closer to a system of self-regulation which can better command the confidence of Parliament and the public as well as the press.

The PCC published in October 1995 a five-point defence of non-statutory self-regulation. It is worth publishing in full:

(1) One benefit of self-regulation outweighs all the others. Newspapers and periodicals are public watchdogs, scrutinising those who exercise power – indeed, that is why a free press is a part of the basis of a democracy.

(2) A free press enables electors in a democracy to make informed choices, for that reason it is crucial to prevent direct government intervention in the press. What would be justified initially as making the press 'behave responsibly' could easily become censorship. Criticism of politicians would be blunted and further restrictions of free expression would follow.

(3) For the industry self-imposed rules are likely to have greater moral force than legal rules imposed by the State.

(4) Compared with legislative restrictions, self-regulation is easily and immediately accessible, fast and flexible in operation, independent of government and the courts and costs the tax-payer and those who complain nothing.

(5) Self-regulatory procedures are informal and involve none of the anxieties which most citizens experience when faced with lawyers and the courts.

Such sentiments do not have universal approval in the publishing industry and are sometimes ignored for commercial rather than public-interest reasons. Cynics frankly admit that they regard as fair game anybody with a story to tell which sells newspapers and magazines. Their critics condemn that approach as one that inevitably will lead to statutory regulation of the media.

THE FACTS

In 1995 (the latest year for which figures were available at the time of writing) the PCC received more than 2,500 complaints. Fewer than 15 per cent of those concerned intrusions into privacy. Of the total number of complaints investigated, only thirty-two were against magazines, twenty-nine of which were resolved or not pursued and two upheld. No breakdown of the basis of the complaints is given but an analysis of the Commission's quarterly reports for 1996 shows that, out of more than 2,300 complaints received, only six were against magazines and none concerned intrusions into privacy.

THE CASES

Journalists frequently have to decide when a private person becomes a public figure, and whether public figures are not, nevertheless, entitled to private lives.

The Royal Family, politicians, people in the arts and entertainment businesses, sports personalities and leaders of public service organisations are clearly in the public eye and their behaviour open to scrutiny by the media.

It is reasonable for journalists to argue that if public figures actively seek publicity to promote their professional aspirations they should not call 'foul' when their private behaviour also comes under the spotlight.

Julia Carling, estranged wife of the then England rugby captain Will Carling, complained that the *Sun* had invaded her privacy by publishing an interview with a former boyfriend, and had given details of a dinner she had had with her hairdresser. She also objected to a cartoon-type sequence in which she was involved in alleged conversations between her and her husband over his friendship with the Princess of Wales.

The newspaper argued that she had previously agreed to interviews to publicise her career as a television presenter and fashion model and that she had put her relationships in the public domain. The PCC rejected her complaint.

But Lord Wakeham subsequently warned the media that the decision in the *Carling* case did not give journalists the right to assume that they were always entitled to give publicity to the private lives of people in the public eye (news story in *The Times*, 8 February 1996).

At about the same time television presenter Selina Scott complained that the *News of the World* had inaccurately and wrongly reported that she had had an affair more than fifteen years ago with a man whom the newspaper had interviewed. She also complained that the newspaper story invaded her privacy without any public-interest justification. In its defence the newspaper supplied the PCC with cuttings from newspapers and magazines either by Ms Scott or containing interviews she had given since 1984 about herself and her career.

The Commission did not regard any of them to be of such a nature as to disentitle Ms Scott from a degree of privacy concerning the reporting of events in her life a considerable time before. Her complaints about intrusion of privacy and lack of public interest under the Commission's code of practice were upheld.

Actor Robbie Coltrane complained that an article headlined 'Cracker's Hideaway' in the *Daily Mirror* had intruded into his privacy by publishing a photograph of his house and identifying where it was. It also included quotes from acquaintances claiming that he had become a very private person whose life had been changed by his partner and young son. The *Daily Mirror* argued that Mr Coltrane's purchase of the property had already been widely publicised and his presence in the village where he lived was well known. They did not believe that in this particular case publication of his address might create a potential risk to him or his family.

In its adjudication the Commission said it was surprised that the *Daily Mirror* had included Mr Coltrane's address in the story, which would not have been impaired if it had been left out, but that it would not censure the newspaper because it had apologised for any distress the story had caused:

The Commission expects newspapers to take care to avoid gratuitously publishing the addresses of people having a public profile.

Conversely, the Commission rejected a complaint by pop star Bill Wyman who believed that *The Times* had invaded his privacy by the 'gratuitous and unnecessary' reference to the name of the street in which he had recently bought a house. He had in the past been pestered by obsessive fans and was concerned that the article in the newspaper would lead to further unwanted attention. He was particularly concerned because his two young children also lived in the house.

The Times claimed that a reference merely to the street in which Mr Wyman lived did not create a security risk such as to invade his privacy and that the roads in which other pop stars lived were well known.

The Commission agreed and the complaint was rejected.

The cases involving Robbie Coltrane and Bill Wyman do raise the issue of how much protection should be given to the privacy of families, and journalists should consider how much damage might be caused to otherwise 'innocent' people.

Three tabloid newspapers – the *Daily Mirror*, the *Sun* and *Today* – ran news stories reporting that a young man was dying of an Aids-related illness. Sadly, there is nothing unusual in that except that in this case the man was the nephew of a particularly unpopular Tory Cabinet minister. The newspapers' arguments that the public was entitled to know that the relative of a senior Cabinet minister was dying of Aids was rejected by the Commission.

TELEPHONE TAPPING

The interception of public telecommunications systems is outlawed under the Interception of Communications Act 1985 but the 'bugging' of private systems is not.

The issue was raised by Labour MP Ann Clwyd who claimed that the use of mobile phones as 'electronic tags' was an invasion of privacy. She said police could pinpoint a person's whereabouts via a mobile phone network to within fifty feet; and, although it was important to crack down on crime, interception without permission was 'like bugging our personal telephones' (news story, *Guardian*, 3 February 1997).

THE INTERNATIONAL DIMENSION

Although the UK does not have statutory privacy laws other countries do, including France, Germany, the United States and Canada, and journalists working on magazines that have overseas circulations should consider the possible repercussions in those countries of what they publish.

However, reclusive twins David and Frederick Barclay, who own the Ritz Hotel in London, lost their claim in a French court for breach of privacy against the *Observer* newspaper and journalist John Sweeney on the basis that the newspaper is sold in France. The court in Paris said the issue was outside its jurisdiction and awarded the newspaper and Mr Sweeney about £2,200 in damages and costs (news story, *Guardian*, 28 March 1997).

OTHER REMEDIES

People who complain about intrusions of privacy are not restricted in their attempts to satisfy their grievances solely by making formal complaints to the Press Complaints Commission. They can seek remedies in other legal actions including defamation, malicious falsehood, copyright and the breach of privacy rights in some types of pictures, breach of reporting restrictions involving young people and the victims of sex attacks, malicious reporting of 'spent' convictions, and breach of confidence, all of which are discussed elsewhere in this book. They can also seek redress under the law of trespass and the infringement of data protection legislation.

TRESPASS

In simple terms, trespass is entering property without permission, but the law provides an implicit licence to enter to certain categories of people, including journalists, who need to go into premises for legitimate business reasons. In such a situation journalists would become trespassers only if they were asked to leave and refused to go. The law allows people to use reasonable force to eject them if necessary.

Complaints about trespass are generally regarded as civil law torts and the appropriate action is to seek a remedy in an award of damages. But the amount of damage done will be negligible and the prospect of journalists finding themselves fighting off actions for trespass is remote.

There is no trespass in observing the behaviour of people on their own property, provided the journalist does so from some other place. Nor is it trespass to 'spy' on people with binoculars or to take pictures of them from some other location.

DATA PROTECTION INFRINGEMENT

If you store information about people on computer you are required by the Data Protection Act 1984 to register as a data holder. In the case of staff journalists this requirement will be met by their employers but freelance journalists who keep that kind of information must make their own arrangements.

The requirement at the time of writing covers only information held on computer, and so journalists who carry out investigative work can protect themselves by recording information in notebooks.

The main provisions of the Act are that information contained in personal data is obtained and processed fairly and lawfully and that it must be accurate and up-to-date. People are entitled to be told whether such information about them is being stored and to have access to it at reasonable times. They can also, where appropriate, have it corrected or erased. However, journalists have the right not to give anybody access to information about them that is stored on computer if that would mean disclosing information about other people.

Three new offences were created by the Criminal Justice and Public Order Act 1994; they are: procuring the disclosure of data covered by the Data Protection Act 1984 knowing or believing this to contravene the Act; selling the data; or offering to sell it or information taken from it. This could have important implications for freelance journalists who make a living selling 'exposé' stories.

Possible tightening of data protection legislation and its likely effect on journalists is discussed further in the glossary.

CHECKLIST

Before publication:

- Has the accuracy of the facts been checked?
- Can defamatory allegations be proven?
- Are you sure that Clause 4 of the PCC Code of Conduct has not been breached?
- Could a defence of public interest under Clause 18 of the PCC Code of Practice be sustained?

After publication:
- Has any complaint has been dealt with speedily and fairly?
- Has the complainant been offered an apology, correction or right of reply, if appropriate?
- Have requirements in cases of a formal complaint been met?
- Has adjudication received appropriate publicity?

A question of morals

12

INTRODUCTION

Whether journalism can be separated from ethics is a long-running argument. Although the line between law and ethics is often finely drawn some journalists assert that nothing and nobody should be allowed to interfere with the freedom of the press and the principle of free speech. Consequently, different codes of conduct and practice have been adopted world-wide in an effort to defend and maintain the principles of free speech, honesty, integrity, truth, fairness, objectivity and privacy.

It is a two-way process: on the one hand, it allows journalists to examine the ways in which they meet their responsibilities, and on the other, it provides the public with a clear indication of the standards they can expect from media professionals and the ways they offer readers to redress their grievances.

The *Concise Oxford Dictionary* defines ethics as 'the science of morals' and an attempt to outline a set of moral principles in human conduct and establish standards of behaviour that are morally correct and honourable.

The fact that some journalists have chosen not to accept those standards or have failed to meet them does not negate the need for codes of conduct: rather, it strengthens it.

Moves are being made to incorporate codes of practice into journalists' contracts of employment, breach of which would be a disciplinary offence. In the real world, of course, many journalists complain either that they work for editors whose motto seems to be: Get the story at any price; or for others where an unwillingness to breach a code rather than to ignore it is regarded as a sackable offence. Ultimately it is a matter of conscience that only the individual journalist can resolve.

Codes of conduct or practice aim to provide journalists with advice on the types of information that should not be published, such as issues affecting national security; the anonymity of victims of sexual attacks (who now have some legal protection); the protection of children from damaging media attention; the need to avoid discriminatory language in reports dealing with race, religion, gender, sexual orientation and so on; and to offer a right of reply to people who feel they have been badly treated in the press.

The main provisions of such codes in Britain are published by the Press Complaints Commission, the National Union of Journalists, the Institute of Journalists and the International Federation of Journalists, and are set out in Appendices 2–5. None is without its critics and the codes are not universally admired by journalists or the public.

Journalists who breach these codes generally face no punitive sanctions, and the public tends to regard self-regulation as an easy excuse for some of the more bizarre antics of certain sections of the tabloid press.

THE PRESS COMPLAINTS COMMISSION

The Press Complaints Commission is an independent organisation established in 1991 with the task of ensuring that British newspapers and magazines 'follow the letter and spirit of an ethical Code of Practice dealing with issues such as inaccuracy, privacy, misrepresentation and harassment'.

It has sixteen members, a majority of whom have no connection with the press: an independent chairman, eight other independent members not connected with the press and seven senior editors drawn from national and local newspapers and magazines. At the time of writing the magazine industry representative was Iris Burton, editor-in-chief, *Woman's Realm* and *Woman's Weekly*.

In 1995 (the latest figures available at the time of writing) nearly 2,500 complaints were received by the PCC and 483 were investigated. Complaints investigated against magazines accounted for only thirty-two. Of those, twenty-nine were resolved or not pursued, two were upheld and one was not.

Complaints about accuracy in reporting are shown to account for the largest share: nearly seven out of every ten cases. Most are quickly resolved to everyone's satisfaction.

Editors are required to take care not to publish inaccurate, misleading or distorted material and to ensure that corrections are promptly and prominently published, together with an apology if appropriate. The Defamation Act 1996 sets out conditions under which the courts can order the publication of statements. This now threatens to place additional pressure on editors to correct mistakes or misleading statements adequately and to apologise for them in a meaningful and acceptable way.

Although the code does not insist that editors must provide a right of reply, it does urge that people and organisations should be provided with an opportunity to reply to inaccuracies when reasonably called for.

Indeed, the majority of complaints to the PCC are resolved directly between staff at the Commission, editors and the complainants. For example, in the quarter July–September 1996 four complaints against magazines were dealt with in that way.

A woman complained to *Bella* that a feature about employers' surveillance on employees, giving details of her disciplinary case, contained inaccuracies and that her picture had been published without her permission. The issue was resolved when the magazine wrote a personal letter of apology to her.

When a man complained to *Elle* of inaccuracies in a piece about the events surrounding his son's murder, the magazine published a correction and an apology.

Similarly, *Just Seventeen* apologised and offered to publish a correction after a woman complained that a photograph of her and her friends appeared in a collage headlined 'Flirty weekend' and that quotes were wrongly attributed to them.

New Scientist published a letter from the director of the Society for the Promotion of Nutritional Therapy following a complaint that an article criticising holistic medicine contained inaccuracies.

THE NATIONAL UNION OF JOURNALISTS

Similarly the Code of Conduct issued by the National Union of Journalists provides that members should strive to ensure that the information they disseminate is fair and accurate and without distortion or misrepresentation. It also asserts the need for prompt and prominent response to complaints, including a right of reply on sufficiently important issues.

PROFESSIONAL ISSUES

Questions concerning privacy and breach of confidence are matters of significant importance to journalists and are delineated in the industry's codes of practice. These issues are discussed in detail in Chapters 10 and 11. Other working practices which do not fit into either of these categories also impose constraints and need to be understood if journalists are to maintain the highest professional and ethical standards.

CONFLICT OF INTERESTS

Commercial considerations in publishing often require journalists not to act in ways that would incur the wrath of proprietors and advertising managers by publishing attacks on individuals or organisations.

Set against this is the need for journalists to be free to present fair, honest and unbiased criticism in order to establish and maintain credibility and the respect of their readers. The result is a conflict of interests. Vigorous, courageous, provocative editorial can help to boost circulations and increase advertising revenue. Bland, uncontentious approaches to editorial content can stunt initiative and dull readers' appetite, leading to a decline in circulation and consequently in advertising income.

Ethical codes require journalists to see the need to resist attempts to impose on them the suppression or distortion of the truth for reasons of advertising or of personal belief or because of threats of legal action.

Additionally, journalists will regard as a reflection on their professional integrity attempts to involve them in the deliberate distortion or misrepresention of the truth by the selective reporting of facts and the omission of potentially damaging criticism.

CHEQUE BOOK JOURNALISM

Large sums of money are often offered by editors to public figures such as MPs, show-business celebrities and individuals who become newsworthy because their personal stories provide entertaining and informative reading.

Payments for information and pictures from known criminals, those awaiting trial or who will be involved as witnesses, or their relatives and friends, should not be made unless there is some overriding public interest and payment is the only way of satisfying this. The premiss is that criminals and their associates should not benefit from their unlawful behaviour.

Remember, also, that prejudicial pre-trial publicity is a contempt of court punishable by fine and/or imprisonment. Kiss-and-tell (or, more pertinently perhaps, kill-and-sell) revelations by former intimates of public figures also need to be handled responsibly, especially when such confidences are on offer to the highest bidder.

WRITING ABOUT CHILDREN

Special care needs to be taken in handling news stories and features involving children. There are strict laws governing what can be reported about children involved in legal proceedings but much human-interest material includes young people who are in the news for other reasons.

As a general rule, children under sixteen years of age should not be interviewed or photographed without the consent of their parents or guardians, nor should they be approached for interviews or photographs while on school premises unless the consent of the head teacher has been obtained.

Children who are involved as victims, witnesses or defendants in sex offence cases cannot be identified by name or in any other way. Even where a journalist is gathering material for other purposes, careful consideration must be given to the desirability of identification and to any likely detriment or damage to the child's welfare.

ACCEPTING HOSPITALITY

Companies wishing to gain editorial prominence in magazines frequently arrange facility visits often to exotic locations on an all-expenses-paid basis. Others offer less-expensive hospitality in the way of lunches, receptions and launches. Editors regard such invitations either as professionally acceptable ways of gathering information or as unethical inducements to favourable editorial coverage. Some editors will decline them, others will accept them but retain the right to make judgements on an event's intrinsic newsworthiness. Impartial and objective reporting is made more difficult in such circumstances and there is a case for disclosing to readers that information was obtained by such means. Television reporting in travel programmes nearly always acknowledges the agents supplying the holiday.

RAISING ISSUES THROUGH READERS' LETTERS

Pages of letters from readers can provide columns of amusing, lively and topical reading. Letters can also be used to bring issues into the public domain in the same way that reporters on local newspapers can approach friendly councillors to raise controversial and confidential issues at a council meeting open to the public. They then become reportable. Such tactics are acceptable only where the public interest requires it.

JOURNALISTS WHO GO 'UNDERCOVER'

The principle that journalists sometimes have to lie, misrepresent and deceive to gather information appears to contradict the requirements of all ethical codes demanding honesty, integrity and fair play. So are journalists ever justified in using subterfuge in their pursuit of truth? The answer is a qualified 'Yes'.

It has long been established practice in journalism that if truth cannot be obtained by conventional means then some 'cheating' is permissible in the public interest. But a distinction needs to be drawn here between issues of public interest and matters that are simply interesting to the public. It is easy (and convenient) to get it wrong.

For example, a journalist who gained employment in a residential home for the elderly to investigate allegations of ill-treatment and fraud would generally be regarded as acting correctly because the public interest demands that such wrongdoing should properly be investigated and, if proven, be dealt with by the appropriate authorities.

But beware of the courts regarding your methods as 'entrapment': that is, so to lead on the targets that they are bound to incriminate themselves. The courts will refuse to allow such information to be given in evidence.

IN THE PUBLIC INTEREST

Public interest is not to be regarded as the justification for all unethical and unprofessional behaviour. It should be invoked to support attempts at discovering and exposing crime or serious wrongdoing, to protect public health and safety and to prevent the public from being misled by things said or done by individuals and organisations.

More than a few journalists and members of the public failed to see what public interest issue was being served when a newspaper reporter and photographer invaded the hospital room of actor Gorden Kaye, who was recovering from major surgery, on the pretext of carrying out an interview with him.

Editors who wish to use public interest considerations to justify misrepresentation and subterfuge for other than genuine reasons could be called upon to explain how such interest was served.

CHECKLIST

Before publication:

- Does your decision to use misrepresentation in gathering information meet the requirements of the industry's codes of practice and conduct on public interest?
- Does the report attempt to give a balanced view?
- Have you carried out checks for accuracy: facts, names, figures?
- Are you sure that the report meets all the requirements of the codes?
- Have you made sure that freelance material was obtained in accordance with the codes?
- Have you responded promptly to pre-publication complaints via the Help Line?

After publication:

- Did you respond to the complaint quickly?
- Have you corrected all agreed inaccuracies?
- Have you provided a right of reply or agreed some other remedy where it is appropriate?
- Have you co-operated with the PCC as fully as possible?
- Did you publish any critical adjudication by the PCC as fully and prominently as possible?

Some pitfalls for sub-editors 13

INTRODUCTION

The importance of sub-editors in magazine journalism is often under-estimated but they play a key role in the editorial production chain, acting as links between writers and readers.

GET IT 'LEGALLED'

Sub-editors must have an even sharper knowledge than writers of the laws that influence what magazines can and cannot publish. Although decisions to publish major defamatory allegations in libel actions making headline news will have been taken by senior managers, after seeking legal advice, too many libellous statements escape the net because of sloppy and lazy sub-editing. Sub-editors should, therefore, have a clear understanding of how and when copy should be 'legalled' and by whom.

Among the major pitfalls into which sub-editors can fall are inaccurate punctuation, careless juxtaposition of words and pictures, misleading headlines, badly cropped pictures with inaccurate captions, wrongful reuse of pictures, and readers' defamatory letters.

Sub-editors must check, check and check again all defamatory allegations of fact in a writer's copy for accuracy and availability of evidence. Query also the genuineness of potentially damaging letters and the writer's qualifications and, again, seek legal advice as soon as possible.

Often the argument against such a process is that it is too time-consuming and costly, but that needs to be set against the potentially extremely expensive and damaging costs of even settling a libel action out of court. A system of 'fact checkers' as employed by some American publications has obvious attractions and advantages.

PUNCTUATION

It can be difficult to read stories that are over-punctuated but badly punctuated copy can cause problems because its meaning is distorted or ambiguous.

Sub-editors must read copy not only routinely for spelling, grammar, punctuation and factual accuracy but also for meaning. A sentence that reads:

Miss Brown returned to the caravan, where she was living with Mr Green

takes on an entirely different meaning when a comma is added after the word 'living'. In the first version it is defamatory of the couple because it states that they are 'living together' in a relationship but are not married. There is no such imputation in the second version.

The sentence was badly written and punctuated by the reporter and the implication totally missed by the sub-editor who clearly did not 'read' it for meaning. A less ambiguous version would have been:

Miss Brown returned, with Mr Green, to the caravan where she was living.

That would have saved one publication a great deal of money in libel damages. Society's views change over time, of course, and it is arguable that to infer wrongly that a couple are living together in a relationship rather than simply sharing accommodation would no longer be regarded as defamatory. But it does nothing to alter the fact that sub-editors should read copy as punctuated and check for ambiguous or misleading meaning.

Care must be taken when adding quotation marks to words such as 'expert', 'honest', 'fair' and so on, because they can carry the imputation that such claims are not believed by the journalist. The statement:

John Brown, the 'expert' in marine insurance fraud, has resigned amid speculation about the company's trading figures

has a potentially defamatory meaning.

Be careful, too, when putting quotation marks around a word or phrase in a headline, especially in court stories. Remember that all allegations should be treated as such until a trial is over – even in headlines.

For example: NURSE 'STOLE DYING PATIENT'S CASH' should not be regarded as legally safe if the statement is unattributed and the trial is still running. The headline is a defamatory statement of fact and the quotation marks serve only to indicate that somebody, somewhere, said those words. They do not prove that they are true, and the defendant might be acquitted. To be safe, therefore, add 'Claimed prosecuting counsel'. It is true that common practice is not to include attribution in headlines on court stories but that does not mean that it is always legally safe.

HEADLINES

There is a belief among some journalists that people cannot be libelled in headlines. That is nonsense. Libel threats can arise out of defamatory headlines based on copy that is legally safe. It depends on whether the text is sufficient to neutralise any defamation in the headline.

In 1994 two performers from the TV programme *Neighbours* complained that they had been libelled in a Sunday newspaper which had published a photograph showing their faces superimposed on a photograph of a man and a woman engaged in pornographic poses. The text made it clear that the performers were 'unwitting' stars of a pornographic game.

They lost their case and an appeal was heard by the House of Lords in March 1995. They commented: 'Whether the text would be sufficient to neutralise the defamatory implication of a prominent headline would sometimes be a nicely-balanced question for the jury.'

Good sub-editors will use their skills, imagination and creativity to write headlines that 'sell' the copy underneath. They will also make sure that those headlines are not defamatory.

One magazine published a factually accurate story about a link between Westland, a British helicopter manufacturer, and a leading Italian aerospace company. The headline read: *Spaghetti Westland?*. It appeared to be an obvious play on the term Spaghetti Western and was, possibly, really quite clever.

The Italian company reacted with 'surprise and indignation' at the headline and claimed it was seriously damaging to its trading reputation and its dignity and, therefore, defamatory. They could also have argued that a question mark in a headline does not protect the magazine from libel nor is it particularly good journalism.

The magazine initially attempted to defend publication on the grounds that the headline carried no such imputation and that it was intended to be merely idiomatic. This approach proved unacceptable to the Italians and the case is reported to have cost the magazine a total of £250,000 in legal expenses.

Another magazine carried a story written by a City Correspondent (presumably not a journalist) about the trading difficulties of a major company in the electrical sector. The copy pointed out that the company had already experienced three years of falling profits and was about to add a fourth. The headline referred to the company as playing 'the recidivist' probably because the copy pointed out that recidivists were 'petty criminals that go on breaking the law no matter how many times they are caught'. It then went on to describe the bad trading figures as a 'crime' (using quotation marks to emphasise the comparison).

Although to a correspondent who is not a journalist the comparison between recidivism and repeatedly falling trading figures might seem apt, a sub-editor should spot it as potentially damaging.

To suggest to some people that a young man who is full of fun, high-spirited and carefree is 'gay' might appear to be a description of his personality; to others it would imply that he is homosexual. A sub-editor reading copy of an interview with such a young man believed him to be gay in the original and normal meaning of the word. The young man's name was Gordon and the urge to head-line the copy as an interview with 'gay Gordon' was irresistible. Gordon later complained that, although he had no argument with the copy, the headline had held him up to ridicule by his workmates because of the imputation that he was homosexual.

The word 'affair', also commonly used to infer a relationship between two people, is best avoided unless a true sexual relationship is intended.

DEFAMATORY WORDS IN HEADLINES

Some words on their face are defamatory because they imply criminal or immoral behaviour. Thief, crook, liar, cheat, drunk, swindle, scandal, fraud, conman: all are examples of words which are attractive to sub-editors because they are short, strong headline words that fit easily across a single column of space. But they should not be used unless they can be justified by the text and then only if the sub-editor is satisfied that the text is accurate.

One magazine ran a front-page story reporting that building societies (only two were named) were putting undue pressure on home loan borrowers by offering them a discount on their mortgages if they would take the societies' home contents insurance policies as well.

The copy made it clear that this was not a crime but the headline referred to it as a 'home insurance swindle', a clearly defamatory misinterpretation of what had been written; the two named building societies could have sued on the grounds that the 'swindle' was being perpetrated only by them.

A SHORTER WORD IS NOT ALWAYS A SAFE ALTERNATIVE

Sub-editors are often faced with difficulties in trying to find words that fit snugly in a predetermined column width and may substitute words which appear to be suitable shorter alternatives. Sometimes they are not.

One common mistake is to use 'sacked' as an alternative to 'redundant'. This shows a fundamental misunderstanding of the difference in meaning between the two. Jobs are made redundant, not people, and to say that employees have been sacked when, in fact, their jobs have disappeared is clearly defamatory because it wrongly implies that the workers have been found unsuitable in some way. You might get away with it when scores or even hundreds of jobs are being 'axed' but not when only a handful are affected and the employees are identifi-able. To headline a story that some key workers were on a company's 'hit list' for redundancy was also held to be defamatory of them.

A magistrate claimed he had been libelled when a headline stated that his 'home' had been used for drugs offences when, in fact, the premises were a house he owned and rented out as bedsitters. The reporter's copy made that fact quite clear. The sub-editor argued that 'house' would not fit in the space available and that 'home' meant the same thing.

None of the above examples is as horrendous, however, as the headline that accused a ladies' hairdresser of rape when the copy said he had pleaded guilty to indecent assault. Inquiries revealed that the sub-editor believed all sexual offences against women were rape.

Particular care must be taken when passing pages for print. They deserve more than just a cursory glance. In hot-metal-setting days, one ill-intentioned compositor changed SEX CHARGE MAN in a headline to SEX CHANGE MAN; on another occasion a well-meaning compositor changed CAR CHIEF to CAR THIEF because the headline was on a (divorce) court story and mentioned a sum of money, and the compositor honestly believed the sub-editor was mistaken.

JUXTAPOSITION OF HEADLINES AND PICTURES

The wrong juxtaposition on a page of headlines and pictures is often very amusing and sometimes potentially damaging. Therefore, it is something sub-editors involved in page design must be aware of and journalists who are responsible for passing pages for print must be on the lookout for.

One page carried a headline reading: SECRETS BASE SCIENTIST MADE OBSCENE CALLS while alongside it was a photograph of a man (not the scientist) with a leer on his face making a telephone call. Another page showed a photograph of a local councillor talking to a group of primary school children over a headline that said: *Pervert pleads to be castrated.*

A national newspaper carried a photograph of the ice skating champion Christopher Dean and his professional partner Jayne Torvill. Alongside it was the headline: *Dean to be tried for adultery.* The news story referred to the Dean of Lincoln and not the skating pair.

Photographs taken for one purpose can often be used for another; then it is not the photograph that is defamatory but the context in which it is used.

A sub-editor on a transport magazine needed a photograph to illustrate a news item about a freight company that had been fined after animals had died on one of its vehicles while being shipped to Sweden. The office picture library did not have a photograph of a truck belonging to the company involved so the sub-editor used a picture of a similar vehicle belonging to another company clearly identified on the cab door.

Similarly, a women's magazine needed a picture to illustrate a feature on child abuse; it used one showing a male model with a little boy that had been used previously with a feature on knitwear for men. The model and the child's parents could have sued because of the defamatory implications that they were somehow involved in the abuse of that particular child.

When a magazine for bikers wanted a cover picture for a feature on leatherwear it used one of a man with one hand in his pocket and the bubble: 'Pocket billiards has never been easier with this generous cut and silky lining'. The sub-editor believed the man was dead and the magazine free from any threat of a libel action. Unfortunately for the magazine, he was alive and well and very angry.

CROPPED PICTURES

If pictures have to be cropped after the main layout has been finalised, be sure to check that the caption does not need rewriting and that any line-up of people in the picture matches the detail in the caption.

WRONGFUL REUSE OF PICTURES

Unless a magazine has a policy of acquiring All Rights on all pictures, sub-editors need to be careful when reusing pictures. If the magazine acquired only First Use (or First European Rights) then it is an infringement of the copyright owner's copyright to use the picture again without permission. This problem is also discussed in Chapter 8. Such wrongful reuse cost one magazine £15,000 in compensatory damages.

Similarly, when magazines publish features based on a newly released book they should not assume that they can use pictures from the book or its cover without permission. Checks must be made on copyright ownership.

Care also needs to be taken when handling pictures provided by public relations agencies and freelance journalists. Magazines have received bills from photographers after publishing pictures that were provided by public relations people who did not acquire All Rights when the pictures were commissioned and, therefore, had no 'right' to send them out for publication in magazines.

The same applies to pictures provided by freelance journalists, particularly those that accompany unsolicited material. Sub-editors should satisfy themselves about copyright ownership before publication.

READERS' LETTERS

It is no defence to an allegation of libel that the defamatory statement was in a reader's letter. For the purposes of libel law, a reader's letter is treated in the same way as a news story or feature. The fact that the reader is giving you a licence to publish it will not protect you if it contains defamatory statements.

Because readers' letters are not written by journalists the potential for them to contain defamatory allegations is great. Those which contain libellous statements will have to be defended by the publishers (and, possibly, the reader too), who could find themselves in the difficult position of having to prove somebody else's claims.

Severe editing of a letter for reasons of space is also fraught with dangers unless you get the writer's permission to publish the edited version. The consideration here is that making substantial cuts in a reader's letter could seriously alter its overall meaning. Sub-editors must be aware that, however savage their cuts might be, they have a responsibility to maintain the balance of any argument.

CHECKLIST

- Are all necessary punctuation marks in place?
- Have any defamatory allegations been identified and legal advice taken?
- Have headlines on court stories been attributed?
- Are all defamatory words in headlines safe?
- Have pages been checked for possible libel by juxtaposition?
- Has copyright been checked on submitted and reused pictures?
- Do pictures and captions match?
- Have readers' letters been read for libel?
- Have cover lines been matched against final content?
- Have copies of content been kept at all stages of the subbing process so that errors can be traced back to the originator?

When a reader complains 14

INTRODUCTION

No editor likes to have to spend time dealing with complaints. A considered and speedy response is often the answer. It can make all the difference between a cost-free retraction and a damagingly expensive trial.

Not every mistake in a magazine is legally actionable. Readers often complain without any justification simply because they do not like what has been written about them, although they cannot challenge its accuracy or interpretation. That is their problem. Other errors are simply mistakes of fact which might upset people but which do them no real harm. These are best dealt with by publishing a correction as quickly as possible.

More care and time must be taken when the allegation is one of libel, malicious falsehood or some other potentially costly claim. In nearly all cases you should take legal advice before doing anything else. Some insurance policies insist on it.

COMPLAINTS BY TELEPHONE

Initial shock and anger at what has been published often stirs readers to pick up the telephone and complain to whoever happens to answer it. The danger here is that if that particular journalist is not familiar with the story he or she will almost instinctively apologise. Even though that seems on the face of it the fairest thing to do, it can be extremely unwise and dangerous because an apology can and will be taken as acceptance of and liability for the supposed error, and this could affect the insurance policy cover. Journalists should always refer to editorial office practice.

Make notes of the complaint but tell the complainant you want confirmation in writing; a letter or fax will do. In the meantime make initial inquiries among the journalist(s) concerned and gather all the relevant material such as letters, documents, notes of interviews, tape recordings. Remember, too, that plaintiffs have one year in which to issue a writ and much can happen to material and witnesses during that time. Notify your insurance company, if you are covered, to make sure you meet its requirements.

COMPLAINTS IN WRITING

Take legal advice, if you have not already done so. Resist the temptation to take what appears to be a fast and cheap way out by publishing, or offering to publish, apologies and/or corrections unless you are absolutely satisfied that the complaint is justified. Even then a hastily put together apology or admission can lead to claims from other people who are named in the copy.

Additionally, staff and freelance journalists might take exception to admissions, arguing that they could have answered the reader's complaints satisfactorily. It could be regarded as a reflection on their professional integrity and has led to claims of libel against editors.

A journalist named Honor Tracy who was employed by Kemsley Newspapers wrote a story criticising the extravagance of a parish priest in Southern Ireland, claiming that the cost of building his presbytery was more than the parishioners could afford. After the priest complained, and without consulting the writer, the editor published a humiliating apology. Consequently Honor Tracy sued for libel and was awarded £5,000 damages.

If, after due consideration, you honestly believe that the claim is without substance then politely but firmly decline to take any further action.

Letters or faxes to the complainants or their solicitors should preferably be written by lawyers and must always be clearly marked WITHOUT PREJUDICE. This allows for an exchange of views without the danger of their being used as evidence in a legal action. Conversations should also be prefaced with the same words. Open letters, that is those not marked 'Without Prejudice', are always available as evidence or for use in cross-examination by either party.

PUBLISHING CORRECTIONS AND APOLOGIES

You will not be able to defend an action against you by showing that you have published an apology or correction if such material has not first been agreed by the complainant or those acting on his or her behalf. There is also the additional danger that by correcting allegations against one plaintiff you unintentionally libel others.

Make sure that the complainant signs a written statement accepting the terms of the apology 'in full and final settlement' of the claim. This agreement must be obtained *before* publication and kept in a secure place.

Questions of wording, headline and positioning of the apology are subject to negotiation but must be agreed in writing beforehand.

PAYMENT INTO COURT

One method of trying to bring a defamation or malicious falsehood action to an end without excessive costs is to make a payment into court. This literally means that the defendant makes a payment into the Law Courts Branch of the Bank of England and gives the plaintiff notice in writing that this has been done. The plaintiff then has twenty-one days in which to take the money or leave it.

Acceptance of the payment effectively brings the proceedings to an end. In actions for defamation and malicious falsehood, however, the plaintiff can apply to a judge in chambers for leave to make a statement in open court to vindicate his reputation, but the statement must have the judge's blessing. The defendant will also have to pay the legal costs incurred up to the date of acceptance.

The difficulty for the publishing company rests on deciding on a sum of money that it believes the plaintiff will accept to discontinue the action.

WHEN THE PAYMENT IS REFUSED

If the payment is refused and the case goes to trial the court will not be told that the payment has been offered until the proceedings have ended and resulted in an award of damages. Prior knowledge of such a payment would indicate to the jury in a libel trial that the defendant had accepted liability but was trying to avoid a public fight, and this awareness could influence the level of damages awarded.

It then becomes rather like a game of Russian roulette. If the plaintiff is awarded the same amount of money or more in damages than has been 'paid in', this has no effect on the defendant. However, if the sum awarded is the same as, or less than, the 'payment in', the plaintiff usually has to pay all costs of the action from the date of the payment in.

This has obvious advantages for the defendant because in normal circumstances the side which loses an action is responsible for meeting *all* the legal costs. Defendants, therefore, who lose cases pay not only the amount of damages awarded, which, in libel cases have been as high as £1.5 million, but also the costs, which could result in a total bill of over £2 million.

IS IT WORTH FIGHTING FOR?

Although you are satisfied that you have a complete defence you should consider whether a settlement is not a better way of bringing the matter to a close.

Settlements are less demanding in terms of time, worry and effort; you could win the battle but lose the war if the plaintiff is poor and cannot meet the costs, and your reputation could be seriously damaged if you are thought to be acting unduly harshly in the circumstances. You could also strike an unsympathetic jury and have to appeal.

CHECKLIST

- Have you avoided an immediate offer of an apology or correction when the complaint is other than a simple non-damaging inaccuracy?
- Have you asked for telephoned complaints to be put in writing?
- Have you consulted your lawyer and insurance company?
- Have you gathered as much information as you can in answer to the complaint before doing anything else?
- If the complaint was without substance, did you politely say so?
- Are your letters and conversation clearly WITHOUT PREJUDICE?
- Have you considered a settlement or payment into court?
- Have you made sure that apologies/corrections are agreed with the complainant *before* you publish them?
- Have you taken extra care to ensure your apology or correction does not affect a third party adversely without their knowledge and consent?
- Have you received a written agreement from the complainants that they accept your action is in full satisfaction of the claim?

What do I do if . . .? **15**

INTRODUCTION

Problems arise in the editorial office of a magazine which cannot always be answered by reference to a text book, or that appear to be of a quasi-legal nature rather than legal fact. Often they are simply questions of ethics and good journalistic practice. This chapter is an attempt to answer some of those questions and to cover other topics of interest not dealt with elsewhere in the book.

SOME COMMON QUESTIONS ANSWERED

I work for an independent publisher which produces magazines for client companies. Some of them try to put pressure on us to publish news stories critical of their competitors on the grounds that they are paying us to do a job for them. So far we have resisted, arguing that it would be we and not the client who would be in trouble. Are we right?

Yes. You cannot argue that you are under pressure to break the law because someone is paying you to do so and thereby escape personal liability. If the critical news stories are defamatory, which you seem to suggest, then the burden of defending them would be yours, and your clients might not have the evidence to back up the claims.

A retailer threatened to sue us because we omitted to mention his company in a list of registered dealers. The mistake was an accident which we admitted and corrected. But could they have taken us to court over it?

It is very unlikely. The retailer would have had to prove that your omission was malicious, that it was done deliberately with the intention of causing him some financial damage; it would be very difficult to prove in the circumstances. If your magazine presented the list in such a way as to imply that any dealer not mentioned was not registered or 'approved' then you could face an action for defamation on the grounds that he was making false claims.

Are embargoes legally binding?

No. You cannot be sued for breaching an embargo because embargoes have no legal recognition. However, people can take steps to make life difficult for you by refusing to send you information in advance of an event, publication of a report and so on. If an embargo falls at an inconvenient time it is better practice to try to get it lifted than to ignore it.

Sometimes an embargo is imposed by contract where, for example, a photographer's admittance to a football ground is conditional on there being no publication before a given time in order to give the 'official' photographer an advantage. This could probably be enforced. However, when a pop group tried to control photographers invited to a photo-call by asking them to sign a restrictive declaration on being admitted to the session, they found that the declarations had been signed, if at all, with false names.

My magazine serves the electrical supplies sector and from time to time we publish lists of between 500 and 600 accredited distributors. We believe a rival is simply lifting our lists and publishing them at a reduced rate but we cannot prove it. Is there anything we can do to stop this?

Yes. One way would be to publish an error that was not serious enough to cause any problems to your readers; another would be to introduce a fictitious company into the list. If your rival's list contains the same error(s) then you have strong evidence that your copyright is being infringed and you can take whatever action you think is appropriate to stop it.

Sometimes people I have interviewed demand to see my copy before it is published. Do they have any legal right to do this?

No. Although it is often wise to allow them to check the copy for factual accuracy, particularly when it includes detailed scientific, technical or financial information, you should insist respectfully but firmly that questions of headlines, layout, writing style and presentation are for the magazine to determine.

My magazine, which deals with personal computers and software products, publishes comparative reviews of various types of equipment and the results are presented as comparative charts, including our performance test results. This obviously has an impact on the overall conclusions about the product. What happens if our test results are wrong?

In exceptional circumstances the manufacturer could sue you for malicious falsehood (slander of goods). For a more a detailed discussion of this read Chapter 7.

If I tested a product and found it dangerous, do I have a duty to my readers to insist that the product advertising is withdrawn?

No professional journalist would give editorial support to advertising for a product he or she can prove is a danger to consumers and any responsible advertising manager would take the same view, but clearly the issue also needs to be discussed with the manufacturer before any final decisions are taken.

Most of the product tests we use are bought from outside organisations and not developed in-house. If we follow the testing procedure rigorously are my journalists still liable for any complaints arising out of critical reports?

Yes, if for no other reason than that you published them. But much depends on the credibility of the testing organisation. If it has a nationally recognised and accepted standing in your industry and you can show that you carried out the testing instructions to the letter, then there is little likelihood of your being successfully sued, because the manufacturer would have to prove malice and that would be extremely difficult in the circumstances. (Read Chapter 7 on product testing where this is explained in more detail.)

Occasionally, when I have been given information in confidence, I have been asked to sign a non-disclosure agreement. Is this legally binding? Could I use the information if I obtained it from another source?

Yes, it is binding if the agreement comes before the disclosure; but if you receive similar information from a non-confidential source you are free to use it, provided there are no other reasons to stop you publishing, such as Official Secrets legislation, defamation and so on.

I am a sub-editor responsible for page layouts but I do not see the advertisements on the pages until the magazine has been published. Recently we received a complaint that an advertisement on one of my pages was libellous. Who would have been held responsible if we had been sued?

Under the terms of the Defamation Act 1996 responsibility would have rested with the editor and the publishing company, but Sec. 4 also states that employees are in the same position as their employers to the extent that they are responsible for the content of the defamatory statement or the decision to publish it. So in this case you are personally in the clear.

As editor of a magazine I received a complaint from a company that we were wrongly using its trade mark in a generic sense and with a lower-case initial letter. As a matter of good relations we apologised, but were they right?

Some trade marks have passed into common usage and are frequently printed as everyday words. However, all owners of trade marks must insist that if mentioned in editorial, their names are printed with initial capital letters or in another distinctive way, otherwise they lose control and, therefore, ownership of the mark which could be a very valuable property.

As a feature writer I have to carry out long interviews by telephone and often record them on audio tape. Do I have to tell my interviewee that the conversation is being recorded?

There is no legal requirement that you inform your interviewees that telephone conversations are being recorded on audio tape although, of course, deliberately tapping someone's telephone is illegal. Recording a telephone conversation is the basis of the working of the answer machine, and no reporter feels the need to tell an interviewee that he is taking notes in shorthand or longhand of a conversation. Most interviewees would assume that some record is being made. You have an additional safeguard, too, if any legal action arises out of information passed on during the conversation, because the tape could be admissible as evidence.

Does using the word 'allegedly' give me any legal protection if I want to publish a statement that is possibly defamatory?

No. If you publish a defamatory allegation you can be sued for it no matter how you try to get around it. The only time the word should be used by journalists is when they are reporting court stories while a trial is continuing, because until the trial is over all claims made by the prosecution, plaintiff or defendant are allegations and not proven facts.

My editor is planning to introduce a page of business and financial news and has asked me to compile it. Although I am keen to accept the challenge I'm a little bit worried because I know very little about the money markets and so on. Can you give me any help?

Obviously you will need a sound knowledge of the City and other financial institutions and also about financial services regulation. A great deal of information can be gathered by knowing how to 'read' the financial pages and understand companies reports and accounts. Such topics are outside the scope of this book, but Scottish Widows and Money Marketing *magazine have produced a booklet called* A Guide to the Art of Financial Journalism, *which would be a good place to start.*

As far as legal issues are concerned, much of your information will be 'price sensitive' and will come from insiders on a non-attributable basis, or it will be based on rumour and speculation. This kind of information is tricky to handle because any suggestion that a company is in financial difficulties or that somebody is acting unethically or illegally is, prima facie, *defamatory. In such cases you would have to rely on the defences of justification and fair comment. You should also bear in mind the possibility that a court may order you to reveal your sources. The Defamation Act 1952 provides a defence of qualified privilege for a fair and accurate report of the proceedings at a general meeting of a public company and this protection is extended (when it comes into effect) by the Defamation Act 1996, which also protects publication of a fair and accurate copy of or extract from some documents*

circulated to members of UK public companies by directors or auditors and
full details are published in the Schedule to the Act on pp. 36–9.

Reports of bankruptcy proceedings are protected by absolute privilege.

Pay particular regard to the requirements of the industry's codes of practice
for financial journalists and personal interests.

A reader complained that a cover line on my magazine was misleading because
it read: 'Win £50,000' but did not indicate that this was the total prize money to
be won and not a sole winner payment. Did they have a case to complain about?

Disgruntled readers can complain to the Advertising Standards Authority
about allegedly misleading cover lines and in such a case as yours the
complaint is likely to be upheld. Other criticisms have arisen out of 'free'
offers of products that in fact were prizes in a competition or involved the
reader spending money at a named supermarket.

Woman *magazine appeared with a cover announcement 'Exclusive! At last,*
the real Anne Diamond'. Instead of an interview with the popular television
presenter, however, the feature to which the cover referred comprised head-
less pictures of eight women (one of whom was Ms Diamond) together with
a 'character analysis' based on their choice of clothing. The publishing
company was fined £600 with £400 costs for applying a false and misleading
trade description to the contents of their product.

A model complained that we had used her picture without her permission in
a feature on women who had suffered sexual abuse as children, and this had
caused her great distress and embarrassment. The photographer who supplied
the picture said the girl had signed a model release form. Was that enough?

Not necessarily. It depends on the uses the release form permits. In addition
to the routine information about time, location, fee and so on, the form should
spell out clearly the actual, anticipated or permitted uses that can be made
of the picture. And, of course, it should be signed by the model.

The Association of Photographers and the British Institute of Professional
Photography publish standard model release forms which could form a starting
point for discussion.

I'm a photographer who attended a one-day law course for journalists, and I
was surprised to hear the tutor say that people could be libelled in a picture.
Was the tutor right? Are there any other legal pitfalls photographers should
know about?

Yes, the tutor was right. It is possible to libel people in photographs,
although the more common cause of problems with pictures is the context in
which they are used. To illustrate a feature on under-age drinkers by publishing
a photograph of children drinking cans of beer in a street in which there is
an identifiable off-licence is clearly defamatory because it implies that the
off-licencee sold them the beer and is, therefore, breaking the law.

Other danger areas to be aware of are trespass – that is, entering private property without permission, photographing children without their parents' consent, and taking pictures in the precincts of a court.

Can you libel someone in editorial on Internet services? Do such services present other problems for journalists?

The answer to the first question is probably yes. No case has yet gone to trial so the question has not been answered by the courts, but in 1995 a scientist who claimed to have been libelled on the Internet was awarded damages in an out-of-court settlement.

However, the Defamation Act 1996 provides a defence to 'the operator of or provider of access to a communications system by means of which the statement is transmitted, or made available, by a person over whom he has no effective control'.

Meanwhile, a Scottish court ruled in October 1996 that the inclusion of the headlines of one newspaper in the Internet website of another newspaper was, prima facie, *infringement of the copyright belonging to the original newspaper (*The Times, Scots Law Report, *21 January 1997). The* Shetland Times *put on an Internet website items from its printed editions. The* Shetland News *also operated a website which carried on its front page advertisements and a number of verbatim news headlines from recent editions of the* Shetland Times. *The* Shetland Times *argued that the headlines were literary works owned by them and that their copyright had been infringed. Lord Hamilton delivering his opinion in court said that was so.*

What should editors bear in mind when considering running promotions and competitions in their magazines, as I am constantly being urged by my publisher to do?

Make sure you are not running a lottery, because they are unlawful under the terms of the Lotteries and Amusements Act 1976. In simple terms you would be running a lottery if you distributed prizes by lot or chance, i.e. first out of the hat, if no skill was required to win a prize and if people taking part had in some way to pay towards a chance of winning. The National Lottery is an example. Normally people who enter competitions have to show some element of skill or merit to win. You could ask them to do that simply by completing a slogan. They must also be able to enter the competition free of charge. If they have to buy your magazine to obtain an entry form then the promotion is illegal. Genuinely free competitions are not caught by the Act. Be careful not to ask them to forecast the results of future events such as a motor race or football match or of an event that has already taken place but the result of which is not generally known.

I am often asked to write editorial to go with advertising campaigns and feel uneasy about it. Is it really a journalist's job? Shouldn't it be left to the advertisers?

Many journalists find themselves in conflict between what their consciences tell them on the one hand and what commercial common sense dictates on the other. Some journalists refuse to write 'advertorials' on the grounds that they disparage their professional integrity; others have negotiated some form of payment by way of cash or 'free' time in lieu, while the remainder write them without any qualms because they regard them as a necessary fact of commercial life – in other words, they make a contribution to their salaries.

But you need to distinguish between advertorials that are published to support an advertising 'theme' such as home improvements, weekend breaks, domestic appliances, which are of general reader interest and without references to specific products, and advertising features that are usually paid for and contributed by agencies to support a sole product advertising campaign and are liberally splattered with product references and recommendations. These clearly should be marked 'Advertising Feature' or 'Advertiser's Announcement' so that readers are not deceived into believing that the product has editorial endorsement of the claims being made for it.

The British Code of Advertising and Sales Promotion, which is monitored by the Advertising Standards Authority, says that all advertising should be legal, decent, honest and truthful; journalists need to keep this in mind when handling that kind of copy.

I often read on the leader and letters pages of magazines a statement that views expressed on those pages are not necessarily shared by the editor and publishers. Does that have any legal effect on the content?

No. Such disclaimers do not exonerate the editor or publishing company from any legal liability for what they publish. They are simply a means of saying that the magazine is prepared to publish points of view which it does not necessarily support.

Making it practical

16

INTRODUCTION

Journalists can now gain national recognition as qualified practitioners by working towards a National Vocational Qualification in Periodical Journalism. The NVQ is open to employees and freelance journalists across the whole range of publications.

NVQs are different from conventional qualifications in that they are competence-based by assessment of how the journalist actually performs in the workplace and not solely by written examination. They are not bound by time-constraints. Candidates work at their own pace to a plan negotiated with an assessor, who can recommend the award of a certificate when satisfied that the journalist has produced sufficient and consistent evidence of competence. As a rough guide it will take up to two years to achieve this level.

CAN YOU DO THE JOB PROPERLY?

Evidence of performance comes directly from the journalist's work itself, usually consisting of a portfolio of published pieces, supplemented by formal or informal questioning. This latter method is particularly relevant in assessing a candidate's knowledge of law and ethics.

NVQs in periodical journalism have been developed by the Periodicals Training Council (PTC), which is the training arm of the Periodical Publishers Association (PPA) especially for journalists working in the magazine industry. However, they are actually awarded by the Royal Society of Arts (RSA) Examinations Board.

ASSESSING LAW AND ETHICS

All journalists working towards an NVQ will be required to show a knowledge of law and ethics. For those working first at foundation level, the elements are defamation, malicious falsehoods, copyright and trespass. For the full qualification in writing and subbing the journalist will be required to produce evidence of knowing the rights and restrictions in reporting courts, tribunals, local authorities and company meetings; contempt of court; defamation and malicious falsehoods; trespass; copyright; breach of confidence; data protection; and trade marks.

In addition, knowledge of all the areas specified in the Press Complaints Commission (PCC) code of practice is required both for the foundation units and for the full qualification. A copy of the PCC code of practice can be found in Appendix 2.

Assessors who are evaluating a journalist's knowledge of law and ethics need to see evidence that the candidate can identify and deal with real problems. It is suggested that such evidence should include notes of any legal difficulties encountered and the way in which they were dealt with.

In some cases availability of that kind of evidence will be limited because of the nature of the magazine, and so the industry has compiled a question-and-answer booklet that can be used by journalists, their trainers and the assessors to provide a more precise account of a candidate's legal and ethical knowledge. A copy of the booklet can be found in Appendix 6.

NOT AN EASY OPTION

This should not be regarded as rote learning and an easy option. The PTC warns journalists:

Certificates for units requiring the above knowledge will not be issued until you can demonstrate the range of knowledge specified to the depth and complexity exemplified by the booklet.

Verbatim answers alone will not be sufficient; you must be able to show by discussion that you understand the principles and application of the knowledge areas covered by the questions.

In its booklet *Law and Ethics for Periodical Journalism NVQ* the RSA Examinations Board aptly states that knowledge of the law is one thing but applying it to the craft of journalism is another. It goes on:

We don't want people who can only pass law exams. We want people who are aware of the legal implications of what they are doing during assignments and take the appropriate action. We want people who can write stories without falling into legal traps. We want people who recognise and consult on situations where they may want to break the law knowingly in the public interest, and we want people who don't put legally suspect headings on perfectly innocent stories.

For a journalist who has been in the job for a considerable number of years and has dealt successfully with a wide range of legal and ethical problems, meeting the criteria for an NVQ should not prove difficult. In other circumstances, where journalists do not regularly encounter such problems or simply sub out any contentious or controversial statements, so that the copy is bland and boring, assessment will prove more problematic. In such cases assessors are advised to use the question-and-answer booklet as an aid to discussion and to explore with candidates potential difficulties and the ways in which they would deal with them.

A GUIDE TO PRACTICAL LAW TRAINING

All journalists who wish to qualify for an NVQ in periodical journalism will need some training in legal and ethical issues if they are to satisfy the assessors that as journalists they have the necessary competence to do the job properly.

The amount of training they get and the quality of it will be tremendously important in achieving that objective, yet in some cases no training is provided at all and in others it is less than perfect.

Students studying journalism at universities and colleges will have their law training timetabled. Trainees and more experienced journalists already working in the industry should negotiate the amount of time that can be set aside for law sessions, bearing in mind the nature and pattern of their particular jobs. The PTC recommends that weekly sessions should be organised and dates set as targets for reaching specified goals. A candidate will need between twelve and forty hours of assessment time to complete the full NVQ.

THE TRAINER'S ROLE

It is not so much the content of the training programme that poses the problem: the RSA question-and-answer booklet provides at least the basis of a training syllabus. It is the way in which the training is delivered that presents difficulties.

Ideally, trainers should be qualified lawyers who specialise in media matters and are experienced journalists. If they are also qualified teachers so much the better. Some do exist but they are few and far between.

Alternatively, trainers can be either experienced journalists who have a solid grounding in media-related legal issues or lawyers who specialise in media law and who have some experience of working in the magazine industry.

TRY SOMETHING DIFFERENT

Whatever the location and qualifications of the trainer, every effort should be made to get away from the conventional lecture method of training, whereby people simply sit as passive partners in the session, towards one in which they are encouraged to become active participants.

This can be achieved by using some or all of the following methods:

1 Visits to criminal and civil courts and to coroners courts where possible. Although the majority of magazine journalists will never need to go to court, a supervised visit will help them to soak up the atmosphere, learn who the various people are and what they are there to do, to see the general layout of a court room, and to be better able to understand the language and the procedure. Writing copy would be an extra but worthwhile task.

2 'Mock' trials in which journalists write short scripts based on actual trials and then role-play the characters involved. When groups are large enough, some members of the group can act out the trial while the remaining members report it. The roles can then be reversed with a different script. Preparing the scripts takes time but once they have been written they can be repeated with other groups.

3 Guidance in how to handle complaints by telephone can also be dealt with by role-playing – particularly important in training with students and in-company trainees, whose initial reaction to an angry reader can often be disastrous. Complaints can be based on those that actually have occurred or can be fictitious, delegates can alternately play the angry reader and the journalist. The trainer can then discuss the scenarios with the groups involved.

4 Seminars are an excellent way of encouraging journalists to work things out for themselves. The trainer writes a number of scenarios based on actual or likely legal problems and hands a copy to each delegate in advance. The length of notice will depend on the particular training location – i.e. college or office – but the class members have to work out their own solutions by the seminar date. When the class meets, members can be divided either into pairs or into small groups, depending on the size of the class, and members of each unit pool their ideas and try to formulate the 'right' solution which they then present to the other groups for comment. The trainer acts as commentator and arbitrator as appropriate.

5 Refresher courses and law up-dates for experienced journalists can present problems for trainers because of the breadth of knowledge and experience across the group. In such cases delegates should be asked to send to the trainer in advance copies of their publications and details of previous law training, together with a note of any particular issues they would like to be tackled.

The session can start either by the course members being given a true/false questionnaire to assess how much they already know (a sample of such a questionnaire is in Appendix 7) or they can be divided into pairs or small groups and asked to prepare a presentation for the rest of the groups on a chosen topic; for example, ten things every journalist should know about libel, copyright, contempt of court, or whatever other issue is being discussed. A great deal of useful discussion arises out of such activities.

6 As much use as possible should be made of real legal problems that have arisen on the journalists' own or other publications using copies of the original cuttings if available. The trainer can then use them as a basis for discussion. It is time-consuming to prepare but well worthwhile.

7 Where the conventional lecture method is preferred, it is useful to allow some time at the end of the session for course members to tackle a number of typical problems. This requires them to apply the knowledge they have been given on the premiss that knowing the law is one thing; being able to apply it in particular situations is another. This has proved particularly successful where the delegates work in pairs or small groups and are encouraged to bounce ideas off each other. They then report back to the whole course and their views are discussed. Examples of questions on libel, copyright and contempt of court are provided in Appendices 8, 9 and 10. 'Model' answers are not appropriate in such cases.

8 Trainers who are asked to provide law refresher courses especially for editors can find some difficulty in preparing suitable material. The course title, 'Law for Editors', presumes there is some special branch of the law that applies only to them.

This is nonsense, of course. In such situations what the editors admit they really need is a general refresher or up-date. However, in-company trainers can include input on the administrative side of law training by suggesting programmes tailor-made for particular groups of journalists, such as feature writers and sub-editors, and by dealing with topics where editors have special responsibility, such as handling complaints, liaising with lawyers, how and when copy is 'legalled' before being passed for print, and so on.

9 A particularly successful visual aid in law training is a video produced by the BBC for training their journalists and called *That's Libel*. It deals with the definitions of libellous statements and the main defences to them; to that extent it does nothing more than require the viewer to watch and listen. But it does end with a number of fictitious scenarios and delegates are asked to express their views on the legalities of what they have seen. There is also an accompanying cassette. The video was produced in the 1980s and some of the programmes used to illustrate various legal points are now no longer being transmitted, but the legal principles it expounds have not changed. It is available from the National Council for the Training of Journalists (NCTJ).

10 A list of names and addresses of some organisations and companies involved in training for NVQs or in media law training in general is given on p. 113.

USEFUL NAMES AND ADDRESSES

Periodical Publishers Association
Queens House
55–56 Lincoln's Inn Fields
London WC2A 3LJ

Periodicals Training Council (at the same address)

National Council for the Training of Journalists
Latton Bush Centre
Southern Way
Harlow
Essex CM18 7BL

PMA Training
PMA House
Free Church Passage
St Ives
Cambs. PE17 4AY

RSA Examination Board
Westwood Way
Coventry CV4 8HS

Appendix 1: Glossary

Note: Every effort has been made to avoid legalese in compiling the Glossary and to include all legal words used in the text as well as those likely to be encountered by journalists in their work.

Absolute discharge	A form of sentence which acknowledges that, although the accused has committed a crime, no penalty should be imposed. The conviction remains on the record until erased under the provisions of the Rehabilitations of Offenders Act 1974.
ACAS (Advisory, Conciliation and Arbitration Service)	Established by the Employment Protection Act 1975 to improve industrial relations and collective bargaining. It is independent of the government and has been called in to mediate during government–union disputes.
Acceptance	An essential element in the formation of a legally binding contract. Acceptance is made in reply to an offer.
Acquit and Acquittals	These terms refer to findings of not guilty of the accused charged with a crime.
Acts of Parliament	The final document passed by Parliament to make the law. They usually start life as Bills; if they successfully get through the procedures during which they are scrutinised by both the Lords and the Commons during the parliamentary year, they become law.
Ad litem	Literally 'for the suit'. A guardian *ad litem* is appointed by the court to represent a party whose views should be heard; for example, an infant or a person of unsound mind.

Administrative tribunals	Not part of the judicial system, but nevertheless making decisions of a legal nature. Examples are the Lands Tribunal, Employment Tribunals and Rent Tribunals. Their decisions are subject to challenge in the High Court.
Adultery	Voluntary sexual intercourse between two persons who are not married to each other and one or both of whom are married. A highly defamatory accusation.
Affidavit	Name given to a document sworn on oath which has the same force as evidence given on oath. In many legal proceedings, affidavits are necessary to support the procedure. For example, to support an application for an interim injunction.
Age of consent	This varies according to the circumstances. In marriage: 16; for heterosexual intercourse: 16; for homosexual intercourse: 18. Campaigns are continually being waged to try to lower the ages of consent.
Alibi	The ability to prove that at the time of the crime the accused was in a different place altogether and so incapable of having committed the crime.
Allegations	Assertions, accusations and charges made in support of or against one party or the other.
Anton Pillar Order	An order obtained from a High Court judge which enables a party to a civil action to enter the other party's premises to inspect, copy and remove documents, including tapes and discs, that might otherwise be removed or destroyed. Of course there are a number of safeguards that may be imposed by the judge, such as the requirement for a solicitor and the police to be present. For obvious reasons, these orders are obtained without the knowledge of the party to be raided.
Arrest	The act of stopping and taking into custody a citizen. Arrests are usually made by police officers but can be made by any citizen who witnesses a crime or has reasonable grounds for believing a crime has been commited, or that a breach of the peace has been or is about to be committed.
Assault	Known both as a crime and a tort. The crime consists of the unlawful laying of a hand on another person, or an attempt or offer to do so coupled with the apparent ability to do so. The tort consists of any act which puts the plaintiff in reasonable fear of a battery.

Assault and battery	The assault element consists of the reasonable fear of a battery, which is the physical attack itself.
Assizes	Prior to the reforms instigated by Dr Beeching in the 1960s, Assizes had been held in England and Wales for the preceding 500 years. They consisted in sending High Court judges on circuits throughout England and Wales three times a year to try serious cases, both criminal and civil, and to ensure that no one was unlawfully in prison. Initially, the last of these duties was the most important.
Attorney General	Principal law officer to the government. Usually conducts high-profile and political cases personally. Almost always conducts the prosecution in treason trials. In certain cases, the consent of the Attorney General is required before court action can be commenced. In others, by entering a *Nolle Proseque* he brings proceedings to a halt. As the appointment is political, it automatically comes to an end when his party loses office.
Autrefois acquit	It is a principle of the common law that no person can be put on trial a second time if they have already been acquitted of the charge. Should a second trial be attempted, the defendant should not plead not guilty but autrefois acquit. Likewise a plea of autrefois convict is made in those cases where a previous conviction has occurred.
Bail	A form of conditional release granted by the courts unless they believe that there is a real danger that the accused will commit further crimes, not attend trial or interfere with witnesses. Refusal of bail can be challenged by applying to a High Court judge. Bail is sometimes conditional on finding sureties. (*See also Surety*) The police also have power to grant bail, and may do so, even before a charge has been made, in order to ensure that persons are available if they are wanted for further questioning or to be charged.
Balance of probability	The standard of proof required for a plaintiff to succeed in a civil trial. It should be contrasted with the standard in a criminal trial, namely, beyond reasonable doubt.
Bankrupt	Persons are declared bankrupt when the court is satisfied that they are unable to pay their debts. They are under a number of disabilities; for instance, they cannot obtain credit, and their assets are controlled by a trustee until they have obtained a discharge.

Bench	Collective name for judges or magistrates.
Beyond reasonable doubt	Standard of proof that must be attained before a criminal conviction is justified.
Bill of indictment	The name given to the document setting out the criminal charges with which the prisoner is accused in a trial by jury.
Binding over to keep the peace	A power by which judges and magistrates require persons before them to behave peaceably without necessarily having to find them guilty of any offence. It is commonly used to stop neighbour disputes getting out of hand.
Blackmail	Making an unwarranted demand with menaces with a view to gain. Because fear of exposure is the prime reason for giving in to blackmail demands, victims who are brave enough to go to the police are granted anonymity.
Bona fide	In good faith; as opposed to *mala fide*: bad faith.
Case stated	A court is asked to state a case for the opinion of another court on a point of law. The most frequent requests are made to magistrates' courts. A case stated consists of a statement of the facts as found and the decision based on them, together with the reasons for that decision. As either party to the litigation, if dissatisfied, can ask for a case to be stated, a defendant may find that his or her acquittal has been overturned if the higher court decides that the magistrates have made an error in law. Thus the maxim that no one can be tried twice for the same offence does not seem to apply; however, as the first trial has been ineffective, the defendant was not in peril.
Central Criminal Court	The crown court for London and a large part of the surrounding counties. It is staffed by a number of judges headed by the Recorder of London and the Common Sergeant. Popularly known as 'the Old Bailey', it has been the scene of many famous and sensational trials. For very important cases, a High Court judge will preside.
Certiorari	An order from the High Court directing a subordinate court to act in a particular way or to arrive at a particular decision.
Chambers	Cases heard in chambers are in private. Formal robes are not worn, and the venue may be either the judge's room

or a closed court room; a notice 'In Camera' will be displayed. Great care must be taken, when reporting decisions made in chambers, that you have the approval of the judge, otherwise you could easily find yourself facing a charge of contempt. In important cases the judge will adjourn into open court to deliver his judgment so that it can be reported.

Chancery Division   One of the divisions (branches) of the High Court. It deals mostly with trusts, wills, administration of estates and company law. It is the division that handles copyright cases.

Chiltern Hundreds   A nominal office of profit under the Crown. As no MP can resign or retire during the lifetime of a Parliament, by applying for the Chiltern Hundreds he automatically disqualifies himself from continuing as an MP.

Circuit judge   A comparatively new creation. Circuit judges sit in both crown and county courts. They are so named because, unlike county court judges who usually sit in one particular court, they are assigned to a circuit of courts.

Civil law   As opposed to criminal law, civil law deals with disputes and regulates relationships between private persons. Of course, the same set of facts can create a crime as well as civil liability. For example, a factory explosion could give rise to breaches of safety regulations (crime) and claims for compensation for death and injuries suffered by the staff (civil).

Committal for sentence   If a magistrates' court finds its power of sentence is too limited having regard to all the circumstances of the crime and the defendant, it commits the defendant to a crown court for sentence. An accused, when asked to elect where he or she wishes the case to be tried, is warned of the possibility of being committed for sentence.

Committal for trial   In many cases, a trial must take place before a jury; in others, both the crown and the accused have a right to choose mode of trial. If there is to be a jury trial, the magistrates must be satisfied that there is a *prima facie* case to answer before making a committal order. At this stage reporting restrictions will probably apply. It is for the accused or, if more than one, for one of them to apply for reporting restrictions to be lifted.

Common law   The law common to England and, later, Wales. From the earliest recorded judgments it is clear that the judges assumed that there was a body of law common to the whole land. Today it is to be found embodied in the case law that has been created over the last 800 years or so. Statute law has in many instances superseded the common law rules but there are still areas entirely dependent on the common law. No statute, for instance, yet prescribes in general terms that a person must pay his or her debts, or perform contracts, or pay damages for trespass or libel or slander.

Computer-generated work Work that is generated by computer in circumstances such that there is no human author of the work.

Confidence When information is received in confidence or in circumstances giving rise to a duty of confidence, then until released from that obligation of confidence by the person imposing it, the courts will act to prevent disclosure or award damages if disclosure has been made. Husband and wife, master and servant are examples of confidential relationships.

Consideration The binding element in a contract that is essential to make it enforceable at law. It must be in money or money's worth.

Contempt of court Conduct that interferes with the administration of justice. It can take the form of disruptive conduct in court, failure to comply with the court's decisions, interfering with witnesses or bringing the judicial system into disrepute.

Contributory negligence When a plaintiff has contributed by conduct or otherwise to his or her own injury. In those cases the compensation that would otherwise be received is reduced to take into account this contributory negligence. Failure to wear a seat belt would amount to contributory negligence and reduce the damages an injured car passenger might otherwise have been awarded.

Copyright The exclusive right to exploit an original literary, dramatic, musical or artistic work.

Coroner Employed by the state to inquire into sudden or unexplained deaths. Coroners can sit with a jury of between seven and eleven persons. They are either barristers, solicitors or medical practitioners, and many have dual qualifications. They have also been responsible for determining treasure trove, but that role is currently being heavily reduced.

County court	The main system of courts administering civil law. The equivalent of the magistrates' court system where 95 per cent of all criminal cases are disposed of. It has a juris- diction for dealing with cases involving up to £50,000. Staffed by county and circuit judges, registrars and bailiffs to serve documents and enforce orders.
Court of Appeal	Various combinations of judges sit to hear appeals from the decisions of High Court judges sitting at first instance, crown courts, county courts, courts martial and various tribunals. The two most senior judges are the Lord Chief Justice and the Master of the Rolls. The other judges are called Lords Justice of Appeal.
Court of Protection	The High Court department which looks after the affairs and property of people who, for one reason or another, are unable to manage their own affairs.
Courts martial	Serving members of HM Forces are tried for most offences, both against military law and the local code, by courts martial which are staffed by three or five officers and assisted by a Judge Advocate General who is a civilian lawyer, usually a barrister. Appeal is to the Courts Martial Appeal Court formed by Lords Justice of Appeal.
Creditors' meeting	A meeting of creditors of a bankrupt person or company in receivership or to be wound up, to decide how to proceed.
Criminal Injuries Board	Set up under the control of the Home Office to consider and to make *ex gratia* payments to victims of crime who have suffered physically or, if dead, to their dependants.
Cross- examination	The questioning of a witness by the advocate representing the other party to the case. The object of the cross- examination is to advance the questioner's case by obtaining agreement to it or by destroying the witness's own veracity or credibility.
Crown	Term used for what, in other countries, would be called 'the state'.
Crown courts	A system of courts brought in to replace the assize system. They have both criminal and civil jurisdiction. There are three tiers. In the major centres of population they have High Court judges, crown court judges and recorders. In the lower two tiers High Court judges do not sit and the jurisdiction is limited to criminal cases.

Crown Prosecution Service	A government-funded service which decides whether to prosecute. Replaces the old prosecuting solicitors paid for by the local police authority. The Service is led by the Director of Public Prosecutions.
Damages	The monetary compensation awarded to a successful plaintiff in a civil action. Generally they are compensatory, but in exceptional cases punitive damages can be awarded. Damages are assessed by judges in all cases except defamation, malicious prosecution and false imprisonment. In these cases, damages are awarded by the jury.
Data protection	During the late 1970s fears were regularly expressed about the vast amount of personal information that was being gathered into data banks and the ease with which it could be transferred, manipulated and exploited.

Despite the UK's being a signatory to the Universal Declaration of Human Rights and the European Convention for the Protection of Human Rights and Fundamental Freedoms, it was not until the government signed the Council of Europe's Convention for the Protection of Individuals with Regard to Automatic Processing of Personal Data that a law became inevitable. The result was the Data Protection Act 1984 which created the Office of the Data Protection Registrar whose function is to create a Register of Data Users, to police it and to monitor the working of the Act with a view to suggesting improvements, and so on.

The Registrar has counterparts throughout the European Union; they maintain regular contact with each other and were behind the recent Directive that will bring further changes to our law within the next two years or so.

At present the Act applies only to records of personal data in machine-readable form: manual records are currently exempt. This position will change.

All data users (persons who hold data) and persons who carry on computer bureaux, including anyone who allows his or her data to be processed by another, must be registered. There are few journalists who do not fall into one or other of these categories; most are in both.

There are a number of categories of persons and activities which are exempt from registration or which do not have to comply with the disclosure provisions. At present journalists are numbered among them. There is a real possibility that the new law will not be so helpful.

The Act at present gives individuals the right to access the record, the right to compensation for errors and the right to rectification. If these were extended to cover journalists' data bases, it would make investigative journalism as we know it almost impossible because any targeted individual could find out what information a journalist had on them and take legal steps to stop the research before the investigation was complete.

Defamation
A tort; a collective name for actions based on libel, slander or malicious falsehood.

Delegated legislation
Acts of Parliament usually do not contain more than the general outline of new law; it is left to delegated legislation to fill in the details. These are usually Statutory Instruments (SIs), Rules or Orders.

Deposition
A statement made on oath for use in court proceedings. In preliminary proceedings all witness statements are recorded as depositions. They may be read at the subsequent trial if the witness is not required to attend.

Diminished responsibility
The plea made by persons whose minds have been affected to such an extent that they are not fully aware either of what they have done or of the consequences of what they have done. A ground for reducing a charge of murder to one of manslaughter.

Directive
Is issued when the European Community makes a decision that requires its members to change their domestic law. Like an Act of Parliament, a Directive does not set out detailed provisions but general principles. The European Directive on the Harmonisation of Copyright resulted in the recent Statutory Instrument extending the copyright term to seventy years after death.

Director of Public Prosecutions
Commonly referred to as the DPP, he or she is a barrister or solicitor who is responsible for the Crown Prosecution Service. Under certain statutes consent must be obtained from the DPP before a prosecution can be commenced. The DPP conducts the prosecution in important trials.

Discovery
A very powerful procedure under which all parties to a case must reveal to the others all the documentary evidence in their possession regardless as to whether it hinders or harms the position.

Discrimination
As the community has become increasingly mixed, so the

need to protect minorities has become necessary. It is unlawful to discriminate, with a few exceptions, on grounds of sex, race, religion, colour or nationality.

Divisional Court   A branch of the High Court, which hears appeals from a variety of sources. It is usually staffed by three judges but can also sit with two.

Domicile   The permanent home of a person or a legal entity. It is of significance in matters affecting tax and divorce.

Duty solicitor   All magistrates' courts now have a duty solicitor who is available to give advice and to represent defendants who are not already represented. There are also duty solicitors upon whom the police can call at night for the benefit of persons charged or taken into custody. The duty solicitors are drawn from a roster of local solicitors.

Employment Appeal Tribunal   Hears appeals from Employment Tribunals. Headed by a High Court judge sitting with lay assessors.

Entrapment   Frequently raised as an issue by way of defence in a criminal trial and by way of explanation in a civil case, e.g. to show that a defamatory situation did not happen of the plaintiff's free will. Journalists must take particular care when using hidden microphones to obtain admissions that they do not say anything that might be considered to entrap the person under investigation.

Equal Opportunities Commission   Responsible for monitoring the establishment of equality between the sexes in the workplace. They support the bringing of test cases as opportunities arise.

Equity   The doctrine developed by the courts to ensure that justice is done despite the rigidity of some of the common law rules. Equity, which was developed in the Lord Chancellor's Court, invented trusts (*q.v.*).

European Convention on Human Rights   Signed in 1950, it created the European Court of Human Rights to enforce and protect the rights guaranteed by the Convention. The UK has been taken to the Court regularly and not many decisions have gone in its favour.

Examination-in-chief   The questions and answers given by a witness when examined for the first time by the party which calls him or her. May only be asked leading questions (*q.v.*) if, with leave of the judge, the witness is deemed to have turned hostile. In cross-examination leading questions may always be put.

Examining magistrate   One who takes evidence to decide if there is a sufficient case to justify sending the defendant for trial.

Ex gratia   As a gift. Many cases are settled by the payment of an *ex gratia* sum. No admission of liability is made, but the expense and anxiety of a trial is avoided.

Ex party   Without the other party being present. Many interim injunctions are obtained *ex party* because the matter is so urgent, for example to stop a story appearing in the press.

Expert witness   A witness called for his or her expertise. Usually both sides have expert witnesses and their reports will have been exchanged to see if, on the ground of saving expense, a common report cannot be agreed.

Fair comment   A defence to an action for defamation. To be successful the defendant must show that the facts upon which the comment is based are true, that the comment is honestly held and that which a reasonable person might hold, and finally that the defendant is not motivated by malice.

Family Division   A division of the High Court. Created in 1970, it is a successor to the Probate, Divorce and Admiralty Division. This new division deals with divorce and other aspects of family law, as well as non-contentious probate; contentious probate is now assigned to the Chancery Division (*q.v.*) and Admiralty matters to the Queen's Bench Division (*q.v.*).

Fine   Pecuniary penalty.

Fraud or deceit   A person must show that he or she acted upon a representation and suffered damage, i.e. loss, and must also show that the person making the representation intended it to be acted upon and either knew it was false or was quite indifferent as to its truth or falsity.

Green Paper   Issued by both the government and the European Commission as discussion documents. They are intended to initiate debate and often lead to draft legislation.

Grievous bodily harm (GBH)   A serious form of assault midway between common assault and wounding with intent.

Habeas corpus   A writ of habeas corpus is issued to summon any person who is holding another in custody to produce that person to the court and to justify the custody.

Hearsay evidence As Dickens related, 'what the Sergeant said' is not admissible as evidence in court. The Sergeant must come to court to say it himself. So a witness cannot say what was said to him or her which caused him or her to act in a particular way. The witness must use words to the effect that, as a result of information received, he or she acted in that way.

High Court Led by the Lord Chief Justice, the Master of the Rolls, the President of the Family Division and the Vice-Chancellor. Sits mainly in the Strand, London, but High Court judges regularly also sit in other parts of the country. Jurisdiction is unlimited. Most libel cases are tried in London.

Home Secretary The Cabinet minister in charge of the Home Office. The department is responsible for all aspects of running the country that are not specifically allocated to other departments or ministries. In particular, public order, the police, prisons, gaming, the Fire Service and the control of aliens are some of the many areas for which the Home Office is responsible.

Hostile witness When a witness called by one party gives evidence which is contradictory to his or her previous statement to the solicitor for that party, an application can be made to the judge to treat that witness as hostile. If granted, the witness can be examined by leading questions to show that a completely different story had been told on another occasion.

Hung jury A jury that is unable to reach either a unanimous verdict or a majority verdict of at least ten to two.

In camera Latin: in chambers. When the judge wishes to hear a matter in private, for example an application for an injunction or some Order involving children, it will be heard *in camera*, that is either in the judge's room or in a closed court room. No report may be made, save with leave of the judge, of what has been said *in camera* without running a high risk of being in contempt. Sometimes during trials in open court, the court will recess into camera to hear particularly sensitive evidence, for example that of an undercover agent.

Indecency Not as strong a word as 'obscene' (*see* Obscenity). The test is whether an ordinary decent man or woman would find the matter shocking.

Indictable offence	A serious charge that must be heard before a judge and jury.
Industrial Tribunals	Established all over the country to hear complaints of unfair dismissal, about redundancy payments, etc. Comprise a legally qualified chairman and two lay assessors, one from each side of industry, appointed by the Lord Chancellor. Procedure is as informal as is possible when lawyers are involved.
Infant	A person is an infant in law until he or she is eighteen years old. Infants are protected by a number of legal rules; for example, an infant cannot enter into a legally binding contract unless it be for necessaries.
Inferior courts	Usually courts with a limited geographical or pecuniary limit.
Injunction	Court order to stop a person doing something or to order them not to do something. In libel cases, the plaintiff will ask for a perpetual injunction to stop the defendant ever republishing the defamatory matter again. Interim injunctions, i.e. those of a limited life, are a constant threat to journalists because they usually come out of the blue just before publication. In defamation cases they will be lifted if the defendant can satisfy the court that he or she will plead justification and has good grounds for doing so.
Inns of Court	There are now four Inns of Court: Gray's Inn, Lincoln's Inn, Middle Temple and Inner Temple. They are all situated near the Royal Courts of Justice in the Strand. They are responsible for calling barristers to the bar and also exercise discipline over their members. It is from the ranks of the bar that most senior judicial appointments are made, although solicitors are now considered for many judicial posts.
Innuendo	A meaning given to words by background facts that is different from the meaning of the words at face value. For example, 'I saw John Smith having a drink in a bar', in the eyes of those who believed him to be teetotal. A possible innuendo would be that John Smith was not very sincere about his teetotalism.
Inquest	Inquiry conducted by a coroner into a person's death.
Insider dealing	Dealing in shares by persons in possession of price-sensitive information by reason of their position or job. There are a number of restrictions, some with criminal

sanctions, that prohibit such persons from taking advantage of their knowledge. For example, company directors of public companies may not deal in their company's shares within three months of the declaration of the annual results.

International Court of Justice
Judicial organ of the United Nations. Sits at The Hague and hears disputes between nations; it decides them in accordance with international law. Its authority is moral.

Internet
The worldwide communication network through computers and telephone links.

Intestacy
A person is said to have died intestate if no will has been made dealing with the estate. In the UK the Intestate Estates Act 1952 applies.

Judicial Committee of the Privy Council
The final court of appeal for a dwindling number of colonies and former colonies. Staffed by senior judges, usually law lords.

Jury
Usually consists of twelve jurors, the exceptions being coroners' and county court juries. The jury is sworn to find a verdict according to the evidence. To be eligible for jury service you must be on the UK electoral roll and between the ages of eighteen and seventy. There are a number of persons who are exempted from jury service, mainly connected with the administration of the law. Unless the case involves highly complex or technical matters or is likely to take a very long time to try, the plaintiff in a defamation action is entitled to trial by jury.

Justice of the Peace
Also known as JP or magistrate: (See Lay magistrates, Stipendiary magistrates).

Justification
A complete defence to an action for defamation. It is necessary for the defendant to prove the truth of his or her allegations.

Keeping the peace
Judges and in particular lay magistrates have had the duty for many years to ensure that the King's/Queen's peace is kept. They achieve this by binding persons over to keep the peace.

Law-Laws
Law umbrella word to encompass all the laws. There is also the popular use to mean the police.

Law Lords
The highest judges in the UK. They usually sit in a committee room in the House of Lords. Their decisions are only subject

to appeal to the European Court. They often sit as members of the Judicial Committee of the Privy Council (*q.v.*).

Law Society Grants the qualification of solicitors and is responsible for discipline and enforcement of professional standards. The Society represents the profession in discussions with Government.

Lay magistrates Appointed by the Lord Chancellor, they are drawn from a variety of persons from a court's locality. It is the intention of the Lord Chancellor to make each bench of magistrates as representative as possible. They are unpaid and do not have to have any particular qualification. (*See also* Stipendiary magistrates)

Leading question A question that suggests the answer, for example: 'Did you have on your pin-stripe suit at the races?', instead of: 'What were you wearing at the races?'

Legacy A gift by will.

Libel A defamatory allegation in a permanent form.

Lord Advocate The government's principal law officer in Scotland.

Lord Chancellor Head of the judiciary. Speaker of the House of Lords. A political appointment, the Lord Chancellor is also a member of the Cabinet.

Lord Chief Justice Senior High Court Judge. Presides over the Criminal Appeal Division of the Court of Appeal.

Lords Justice of Appeal Preside over the various divisions of the Court of Appeal.

Lottery Any distribution of prizes by lot or chance. Illegal unless participation in the lottery is absolutely free or the lottery is specifically exempted by legislation.

Magistrates *See* Lay magistrates; Stipendiary magistrates.

Magistrates' clerk Responsible for the administration of the court. Legally qualified and therefore advises the Bench if asked to do so on matters of law. They must not advise the Bench on questions of fact.

Magistrates' courts The work horse of the criminal justice system in this country: 95 per cent of all criminal cases are heard and completed in these courts. In addition to their criminal work, they also deal with a limited number of civil matters, such as husband and wife disputes, extension of licensing hours, neighbour disputes likely to involve breaches of the peace, and destruction of dangerous dogs.

Malice

The element that a plaintiff must show in order to defeat a defence of qualified privilege or fair comment to an action for defamation, and also the necessary element that the plaintiff must prove in a claim for malicious falsehood. It consists of active ill will, or complete disregard for the truth, or acting with an ulterior purpose or motive.

Malicious falsehood

Another name for Trade libel.

Mandamus

A command from the High Court requiring a person to do some act.

Manslaughter

The unlawful killing of another but without the necessary intention that would otherwise make the charge one of murder. The intent that makes manslaughter into murder is 'malice aforethought'. The House of Lords in 1985 laid down that the defendant must have actually foreseen that death or grievous bodily harm was a natural result of what he was doing. The case involved two drunken men playing a game with shotguns. There are a number of statutory exceptions reducing murder to manslaughter.

Master of the Rolls

Head of the Civil Division of the Court of Appeal. Appeals from interim injunction orders are usually heard by the Master of the Rolls.

Mens rea

Latin: Guilty mind. A necessary element in every criminal offence unless it is one of strict liability. The prosecution must prove this element, i.e. that the defendant did the act knowing it was wrong, or alternatively not caring whether it was wrong or not.

Misdirection

It is often alleged in grounds for appeal that the judge had misdirected either the jury or himself on a matter of fact or law. Misdirection equals a mistake in this context.

Mitigation

A plea in mitigation is made following a plea of guilty or a finding of guilty in order to persuade the magistrate or judge that the penalty should be as merciful as possible. If the plea involves slurs on third parties, great care must be taken in reporting these as the court may have made an order under sec. 58 of the Criminal Procedure and Investigations Act 1996.

Monopolies and Mergers Commission	Considers matters referred to it by the Director General of Fair Trading and appropriate government departments and reports on whether a particular situation is or is likely to become against the public interest. Mergers of media companies have been so referred.
Moral rights	Introduced into UK law by the Copyright Act 1988. They consist of the right of every author to have his or her work attributed to him or her and that the work shall not be treated in a derogatory way. The author must claim the right to recognition, but need only claim it once. Moral rights last as long as copyright. There are exceptions to the rigour of the rights in respect of publication in newspapers and magazines.
Murder	An unlawful act or omission causing death amounts to murder if it is promoted by an intention to kill or cause grievous bodily harm (whether to the person killed or to another).
Negligence	The failure to meet a presupposed duty of care. The standard of care that is required varies according to the circumstances. Thus the degree of care and expertise required of a specialist surgeon is much higher than of a GP performing the same surgical procedure. The standard of care is also measured by what was considered good practice at the time the alleged breach occurred.
No case to answer	The submission made after the prosecution or plaintiff have completed their evidence. It denotes that, even unchallenged, there is insufficient material to support the charge or claim. If successful, judgment will be entered for the defendant.
Nominal damages	A small sum awarded to denote that breach of the law has occurred. In a defamation action, a jury will be directed that, if they think that the plaintiff has been defamed but that no damage has been done to his or her reputation, they should consider awarding nominal damages, usually the smallest coin of the realm. Such an award may disentitle the plaintiff to his costs.
Null and void	Of no legal effect.
Obiter dicta	Statements or reasons made by a judge when giving judgment that were not strictly necessary for the decision. Accordingly, these statements or reasons may be disregarded when considering the judgment in later cases.

Obscenity	Defined by the Obscene Publications Act as words which, taken as a whole, would tend to deprave or corrupt those who are likely, having regard to all the circumstances, to read them.
Offer	Essential ingredient of a legally binding agreement. The offer must be unconditional.
Official Receiver	Appointed to manage bankruptcies and winding-ups where no other party can be found to take over the business because the assets are so limited.
Official secrets	There is a series of Official Secrets Acts. Those who take employment under the Crown must sign a document whereby they are bound not to disclose information acquired during their service.
Old Bailey	The nickname for the crown court for London, which is situated at the junction of Newgate Street, Holborn Viaduct and Old Bailey.
Ombudsmen	Act as referees deciding between claimants and their industrial opponents. There are now many ombudsmen serving different industries. The name comes from Scandinavia, where the idea originated.
Open verdict	May be returned when the cause of death at an inquest cannot be determined.
Pardon	Granted by the Crown to a convicted person on the advice of the Home Secretary.
Parliamentary Counsel	A department consisting of barristers who are responsible for drafting legislation for government and, on occasion, for private individuals.
Passing off	Putting on to the market goods that, because of their name or packaging or marketing, so resemble another as to confuse the purchasing public into believing that they are really buying the other goods. In a recent case, the court stopped a well-known supermarket selling their own-brand biscuits under the name 'Puffin' because of confusion with the well-known brand 'Penguin'.
Patent	Protects an invention, i.e. the way to make an article. It does not protect the idea itself. For example, patenting your mouse trap does not give you control over the idea of a mouse trap.

Payment into court	Defendants who wish to bring an action to an end can make a payment into court with or without a denial of liability. The result is that if at the end of the day the plaintiff recovers the same or less in damages then he or she will probably have to pay the defendant's legal costs after the date of payment.
Perjury	Speaking or knowingly making a false statement on oath.
Plaintiff	The person bringing an action for redress in a civil court.
Post mortem	Latin: after death. A post mortem is conducted to ascertain or confirm the cause of death. If an inquest (*q.v.*) is held, the person who conducted the post mortem will give evidence.
Precedent	A doctrine of the common law: indeed, its foundations are built on precedents. A precedent is a decision of a competent court which will be followed by all inferior courts until it is either overruled by a superior court decision or by Act of Parliament.
Pre-trial review	A system introduced into the county courts by which, at an early stage, the Registrar reviews the case and pleadings in order to make such orders as are necessary for the fair and speedy disposal of the case. The system is now used extensively throughout the legal system.
Printer's imprint	Since the middle of the nineteenth century, every printed paper, with a few limited exceptions, must carry a printer's imprint if printed in the UK, giving the name and address of the printer.
Privilege	Occasions when the law, on grounds of public policy, recognises that the ordinary legal rules should not apply. So MPs are privileged when they speak in the House. Communications between husband and wife and between solicitor and client are also privileged. (*See also* Qualified privilege.)
Probate	A grant of probate must be applied for by the executors of a will. When granted, they have authority to manage the estate and to distribute it according to the will.
Proof	The legal name given to a witness statement when it has been taken by a solicitor.
Public interest	The law recognises that there are occasions when private rights must give way to the public interest, i.e. the good of the majority. Unfortunately, there is no straightforward

defence open to the press that publication was in the public interest.

Qualified privilege	A possible defence to an action for defamation.
Queen's Bench Division	A division of the High Court whose jurisdiction in civil matters is unlimited as to amount. It is in this Division that actions for defamation are tried.
Queen's Counsel	A senior barrister of at least ten years' standing, whose practice justifies the step, may apply to the Lord Chancellor to take silk, i.e. to become a Queen's Counsel. If he or she is successful, they will no longer draft pleadings or do interlocutory work.
Queen's Proctor	Investigates the circumstances of a divorce petition or argues a difficult point of divorce law when the court wishes. The Queen's Proctor may also initiate investigations if between the decree nisi and the decree absolute there is reason to do so.
Rape	Sexual intercourse obtained by force or deception. There are a number of special reporting restrictions in rape cases.
Ratio decidendi	The principle upon which the decision in a case is based. It is not always easy to determine the *ratio decidendi* and sometimes the judge may give more than one.
Real property	For practical purposes this means land.
Receiver	The person appointed to look after the assets of a bankrupt.
Recognisance	An undertaking on pain of forfeiting a sum of money to appear on a designated date or to be of good behaviour.
Redundancy payments	Compensation set by statute to be paid to employees of two years' standing (a period currently under pressure to be reduced) whose jobs disappear owing to a reorganisation or closure of a department.
Rehabilation of Offenders Act 1974	Greatly improves the old common law rule that a man could be allowed to forget a past offence after leading a blameless life for many years. It sets out a timescale after which a person convicted of an offence could forget it for all purposes. There are special provisions for allowing the publication of spent convictions.
Respondent	The person against whom a petition is brought and also the defendant to an appeal.

Restrictive trade practices	All agreements that have either overtly or by necessary implication restrictive elements affecting third parties must be registered. It is the duty of the Restrictive Trade Practices Registrar to review them and put before the court any that appear unacceptable. The parties must then either abandon them or satisfy the court that they are in the public interest.
Royal Assent	The signature on behalf of the Sovereign to an Act of Parliament which enables it to become law.
Security for costs	May at any time be ordered by the court. It is often ordered when one of the parties is resident abroad. It is sometimes made a condition for granting leave to appeal. Security means that a sum of money has to be lodged in court so that, if the party ordered to give security loses the case, there is a fund from which the other party can be paid.
Setting down an action	The moment when a civil case becomes live for the purpose of the Contempt of Court Act 1981. It is the time when the plaintiff applies for a trial date.
SI	*See* Statutory Instrument.
Slander	Defamatory material in a non-permanent form.
Slander of goods	An aspect of malicious falsehood; it is a false, damaging and malicious statement about someone's goods.
Solicitor	A person who has passed the qualifing examinations and been admitted to the roll of solicitors. A practising certificate is also necessary in order to practise. Solicitors are usually the first point of contact for the layman involved in legal problems. It is through a solicitor that a barrister may be consulted.
Special damages	Amounts of damages that can be quantified, such as loss of wages or the cost of replacing damaged clothes or the cost of repair to a car, that should be pleaded and which are recoverable in addition to general damages.
Spent convictions	Regarded as 'erased' by virtue of the Rehabilitation of Offenders Act.
Standards of proof	In a criminal case: beyond reasonable doubt. In a civil case: on the balance of probabilities.
Statute	An Act of Parliament.
Statutory Instrument	Secondary legislation providing the detail not included in the relevant statute.

Stay of execution	An application to delay enforcement of a court's judgment or order. It is often granted on such terms as that notice of appeal shall be entered within a specified number of days.
Sting	The damaging allegation in a defamatory statement.
Stipendiary magistrates	Employed magistrates, either barristers or solicitors who usually sit alone and have the same powers as two lay magistrates. They are only to be found in large cities where the volume of work makes the need for full-time magistrates necessary. The Chief Magistrate, who is a stipendiary magistrate, sits at Bow Street Court. (*See also* Lay magistrates.)
Striking off	The removal of a solicitor from the Roll. Barristers are disbarred. Although these procedures most frequently happen as a result of misdemeanour, they can occur for purely innocent reasons, for example, because the individual wants to change profession.
Striking out	The procedure whereby a party to a civil action applies to a court to have part or the whole of the opponent's pleading removed. Reasons could be that it shows no cause of action or that it is irrelevant to the claim.
Sub judice	When a matter is before the court comment on it is restricted because it is said to be *sub judice*. Any comment runs the risk of being in contempt of court, so great care must be taken, particularly if the case is before a jury.
Summing up	A review by the judge, at the end of the evidence and after the closing speeches, of the evidence relevant to the issues, directions as to the law and finally a direction as to the degree of proof required to reach a verdict.
Surety	A common condition for the granting of bail. A surety is a person of good standing who agrees to forfeit a sum of money if the defendant fails to attend court to stand trial. If the surety fears that the defendant will not appear then he or she should apply immediately to the court to be released.
Tape recordings	Audio tapes are admissible as evidence, provided they can be shown to be unadulterated and genuine. In some cases recorders are used to trap the guilty. Great care must be taken to ensure entrapment is not involved. Tape recorders must not be used in court without the leave of the judge.

Tipstaff	The High Court official responsible for seeing that all High Court judges' orders and decisions are carried out.
Title	Proof, usually in documentary form, that a person is the true owner of a property.
Tort	Norman French: wrong. It is the label given by lawyers to most civil actions which are not based on contract. Defamation is a tort.
Trade description	Any description of the origin and/or characteristics of goods. Anyone who applies a false trade description to goods or supplies goods to which a false trade description has been applied commits a criminal offence. The description has to be false to a material degree. A cover line has been held to be a trade description.
Trade mark	It is private property. To be protected a trade mark must be registered and the owner must not let it fall into common parlance and become generic. Journalists should protect trade marks by giving them a capital letter or other distinguishing feature.
Trade names	May, like trade marks, be claimed as private, but can only be protected by an action for passing off unless they are a copyright artistic work.
Trespass	Any interference with property or land which is in the possession of another.
Trust	A device by which property can be held for the benefit of others on specified terms that ensure the capital sums do not come under the control of the beneficiaries, except under the terms of the trust.
Typographical arrangements	Protected by copyright law for twenty-five years from first publication. The copyright belongs to the publisher.
Unfair dismissal	Claims are taken to employment tribunals. In cases involving breach of contract they could also be brought in the county court or the High Court.
Unlawful	Contrary to law.
Verdict	The jury's answer to the question they have been asked to consider. In a defamation action the answer will include an award of damages if they find for the plaintiff.
Vicarious liability	Liability for another's actions. Arises because of a pre-existing relationship such as master and servant, principal

and agent, or, in certain circumstances, husband and wife.

Vice-Chancellor   Head of the Chancery Division of the High Court.

Waiver   Voluntarily giving up a claim. May be absolute or conditional. Under copyright law, waivers of moral rights must be made in writing and signed by the author.

Warrant   The document issued by a magistrates' court ordering a named person's arrest, often backed by bail, i.e. containing the bail requirements to avoid keeping the person in custody.

Witness   Person giving evidence. As there are many conditions that may be imposed on the reporting of a witness's evidence, care must be used to ensure that any conditions are complied with. A husband and wife cannot be compelled to give evidence against each other.

Writ   The document issued by the court to institute an action.

Youth court   The successor to juvenile courts. Tries offenders between the ages of ten and seventeen inclusive, unless the offence or the fact that the young person is jointly tried with an adult requires trial at an adult court. There are very severe restrictions on reporting cases heard in youth courts.

Appendix 2:
Press Complaints Commission Code of Practice

At the time of going to press, the Code of Practice for Newspaper and Magazine Publishing was being revised in the light of the circumstances of Princess Diana's death. We have been given permission to publish a draft of the proposed new code but, as it had not been finally agreed on at the time of going to press, readers should obtain a definitive version from the Press Complaints Commission. Indeed, as all codes are regularly updated in the light of experience, readers should regularly apply for the current version to ensure that they keep right up to date.

The Press Complaints Commission is charged with enforcing the following Code of Practice which was framed by the newspaper and periodical industry and ratified by the Press Complaints Commission. All members of the press have a duty to maintain the highest professional and ethical standards. This code sets the benchmarks for those standards. It both protects the rights of the individual and upholds the public's right to know. The code is the corner-stone of the system of self regulation to which the industry has made a binding commitment. Editors and publishers must ensure that the Code is observed rigorously not only by their staff but also by anyone who contributes to their publications. It is essential to the workings of a voluntary code that it be honoured not only to the letter but in the full spirit. The Code should not be interpreted so narrowly as to compromise its commitment to respect the rights of the individual, nor so broadly that it prevents publication in the public interest. It is the responsibility of editors to co-operate as swiftly as possible in PCC enquiries. Any publication which is criticised by the PCC under one of the following clauses must print the adjudication which follows in full and with due prominence.

1. Accuracy
i) Newspapers and periodicals should take care not to publish inaccurate, misleading or distorted material including pictures.

ii) Whenever it is recognised that a significant inaccuracy, misleading statement or distorted report has been published, it must be corrected promptly and with due prominence.

iii) An apology must be published whenever appropriate.

iv) A newspaper or periodical must always report fairly and accurately the outcome of an action for defamation to which it has been a party.

v) Newspapers, whilst free to be partisan, must distinguish clearly between comment, conjecture and fact.

2. Opportunity to reply

A fair opportunity to reply to inaccuracies must be given to individuals or organisations when reasonably called for.

*3. Privacy

i) Everyone is entitled to respect for his private and family life, his home, health and his correspondence. A publication will be expected to justify intrusions into any individual's private life without consent.

ii) The use of longlens photography to take pictures of people in private places without their consent is unacceptable.

Note – Private places are defined as private property or places where people may have reasonable expectation of being private.

*4. Harassment

i) Journalists and photographers must neither obtain nor seek to obtain information or pictures through intimidation, harassment or persistent pursuit.

ii) They must not photograph individuals in private places (as defined in the note to Clause 3) without their consent; must not persist in telephoning, questioning, pursuing or photographing individuals after having been asked to desist; must not remain on their property after having been asked to leave and must not follow them.

iii) Editors must ensure that those working for them comply with these requirements and must not publish material from other sources which does not meet these requirements.

5. Intrusion into grief or shock

In cases involving grief or shock, enquiries should be carried out and approaches made with sympathy and discretion. Publication of stories at such a time must also normally be undertaken with due discretion.

6. Children

i) Journalists must not interview or photograph children under the age of 16 on subjects involving the welfare of the child or of any other child, in the absence of or without the consent of a parent or other adult who is responsible for the children.

ii) Pupils must not be approached or photographed while at school without the permission of the school authorities.

iii) There must be no payment to minors for material involving the welfare of children nor payment to parents or guardians for material about their children or wards.

iv) Where material about the private life of a child is published, there must be justification for publication other than the relationship with one or both parents or guardian.

7. Children in sex cases

1. The press must not, even where the law does not prohibit it, identify children under the age of 16 who are involved in cases concerning sexual offences, whether as victims, or as witnesses or defendants.

2. In any press report of a case involving a sexual offence against a child:
   i)   The child must not be identified.
   ii) The adult should be identified.
   iii) The word 'incest' must not be used where a child victim might be identified.
   iv) Care must be taken that nothing in the report implies the relationship between the accused and the child.

*8. Listening devices

Journalists must not obtain or publish material obtained by using clandestine listening devices or by intercepting private telephone conversations.

*9. Hospitals

i) Journalists or photographers making enquiries at hospitals or similar institutions must identify themselves to a responsible executive and obtain permission before entering non-public areas.

ii) The restrictions on intruding into privacy are particularly relevant to enquiries about individuals in hospitals or similar institutions.

10. Innocent relatives and friends

Unless it is contrary to the public's right to know, the press must generally avoid identifying relatives or friends of persons convicted or accused of crime.

*11. Misrepresentation

i)   Journalists must not generally obtain or seek to obtain information or pictures through misrepresentation or subterfuge.

ii) Documents or photographs should be removed only with the express consent of the owner.

iii) Subterfuge can be justified only in the public interest and only when material cannot be obtained by any other means.

12. Victims of sexual assault

The press must not identify victims of sexual assault or publish material likely to contribute to such identification unless there is adequate justification and, by law, they are free to do so.

13. Discrimination

i) The press must avoid prejudicial or pejorative reference to a person's race, colour, religion, sex or sexual orientation or to any physical or mental illness or handicap.

ii) It must avoid publishing details of a person's race, colour, religion, sex or sexual orientation unless these are directly relevant to the story.

14. Financial journalism

i) Even where the law does not prohibit it, journalists must not use for their own profit financial information they receive in advance of its general publication, nor should they pass such information to others.

ii) They must not write about shares or securities in whose performance they know that they or their close families have a significant financial interest without disclosing the interest to the editor or financial editor.

iii) They must not buy or sell, either directly or through nominees or agents, shares or securities about which they have written recently or about which they intend to write in the near future.

15. Confidential sources

Journalists have a moral obligation to protect confidential sources of information.

*16. Payment for articles

i) Payment or offers of payment for stories, pictures or information must not be made directly or through agents to witnesses or potential witnesses in current criminal proceedings or to people engaged in crime or to their associates – which include family, friends, neighbours and colleagues – except where the material concerned ought to be published in the public interest and the payment is necessary for this to be done.

* There may be exceptions to the clauses marked * where they can be demonstrated to be in the public interest

1. The public interest is defined as:
   i)   Detecting or exposing crime or a serious misdemeanour.
   ii) Protecting public health and safety.
   iii) Preventing the public from being misled by some statement or action of an individual or organisation.

2. In any case where the public interest is invoked, the Press Complaints Commission will require a full explanation by the editor demonstrating how the public interest was served.

3. In cases involving children, the public interest must be overriding (see Clause 6).

Appendix 3:
National Union of Journalists Code of Conduct

1. A journalist has a duty to maintain the highest professional and ethical standards.

2. A journalist shall at all times defend the principle of the freedom of the press and other media in relation to the collection of information and the expression of comment and criticism. He/she shall strive to eliminate distortion, news suppression and censorship.

3. A journalist shall strive to ensure that the information he/she disseminates is fair and accurate, avoid the expression of comment and conjecture as established fact and falsification by distortion, selection or misrepresentation.

4. A journalist shall rectify promptly any harmful inaccuracies, ensure that corrections and apologies receive due prominence and afford the right of reply to persons criticised when the issue is of sufficient importance.

5. A journalist shall obtain information, photographs and illustrations only by straightforward means. The use of other means can be justified only by overriding considerations of the public interest. The journalist is entitled to exercise a personal conscientious objection to the use of such means.

6. Subject to the justification by overriding considerations of the public interest, a journalist shall do nothing which entails intrusion into private grief and distress.

7. A journalist shall protect confidential sources of information.

8. A journalist shall not accept bribes nor shall he/she allow other inducements to influence the performance of his/her professional duties.

9. A journalist shall not lend himself/herself to the distortion or suppression of the truth because of advertising or other considerations.

10. A journalist shall mention a person's age, sex, race, colour, creed, illegitimacy, disability, marital status, or sexual orientation only if this information is strictly relevant. A journalist shall neither originate nor process material which encourages discrimination, ridicule, prejudice or hatred on any of the above-mentioned grounds.

11. A journalist shall not take private advantage of information gained in the course of his/her duties before the information is public knowledge.

12. A journalist shall not by way of statement, voice or appearance endorse by advertisement any commercial product or service save for the promotion of his/her own work or of the medium by which he/she is employed.

Appendix 4:
Institute of Journalists Code of Professional Ethics

SCHEDULE I

Code of Professional Ethics

1 The Institute believes that the Press and all other media of mass communication have a vital part to play in society by providing information and comment on matters of public concern. To discharge this duty effectively they must be free, but freedom being liable to abuse brings its own responsibilities. Moreover, examples however isolated, of any but the highest standards of journalism reflect on the medium concerned and by bringing it into disrepute lessen the confidence of the public and invite the imposition of controls.

2 The Institute fully recognises the competitive and other pressures to which journalists are subject, but emphasises the personal responsiblity of every member for the material that he gathers, prepares or publishes and the methods used in so doing.

3 Every Member is therefore required to subscribe to the code contained in this schedule which stipulates that the following acts are discreditable to a journalist thereby carrying the penalties prescribed in Bye-law 26:

(a) The expression of comment or conjecture as established fact, or the submission of deliberately inaccurate or distorted stories including those in which essential facts are knowingly supressed.

(b) The obtaining of news or pictures by misrepresentation (save where important information of legitimate public interest can be obtained in no other way) or by any other form of dishonesty whatsoever, by intimidation or by undue intrusion on privacy.

(c) Failure to rectify spontaneously and promptly harmful inaccuracies in published information so soon as discovered or brought to notice.

(d) The publication of corrections or apologies in such a form or in such a position that they do little or nothing to counteract the impression made by the original story.

(e) The refusal to afford a reasonable opportunity to reply to those who have been criticised.

(f) The identification in relation to the proceedings before a court or tribunal of relatives or other persons not directly involved in such proceedings save when such identification is of legitimate public interest.

(g) Failure to honour confidences received in the course of professional activity.

(h) Writing or altering editorial copy at the request of an advertiser or in exchange for advertising or any other consideration, taking or altering news feature pictures at the request of an advertiser or in exchange for advertising or any other consideration, or offering to do so, except for use in clearly marked advertising pages or supplements.

(i) Abuse, for personal gain, either immediate or contemplated, of opportunities afforded by professional duties to influence the investment decisions of members of the public, or abuse for the same purpose of knowledge gained in the course of professional activities.

SCHEDULE II

Professional Usage and Practice

1   It is recognised by the Institute –
(a) That all journalists in a correspondence district have an equal professional right to send correspondence from that district to any journal or agency which has not already a recognised correspondent in the district.

(b) That correspondents should be chosen from among recognised journalists whose ordinary occupation is in the active collection of news for the Newspaper Press or Broadcasting media.

(c) That a journalist who is appointed by a journal or agency as its correspondent in a district has an exclusive title to send all ordinary correspondence from such district to that journal or agency and this principle applies where two or more journalists work in common in supplying news or correspondence to particular journals and agencies.

(d) That in cases of delegation of duty in the supplying of correspondence, fair remuneration, at the rate of not less that 50 per cent of the proceeds, should be given to the journalist who does the work so delegated. However, it is deemed unprofessional for any correspondent to delegate his work except for temporary and exceptional purposes.

2   Any of the acts or proceedings hereinafter named or described may be deemed to be an act or default discreditable to a journalist, viz:
(a) The supply of false news or exaggerated reports.

(b) Using for correspondence, lineage, or otherwise, the copy of any journalist, whether in proof or manuscript, without the consent previously received of such journalist.

(c) The sending of speculative correspondence in ordinary general news to any journal or agency from a correspondence district other than his own district, in which there is in active practice an accredited local journalist or journalists.

(d) Sending from his own correspondence district general news to any journal or agency which already has in that district an accredited correspondent, but this clause shall not be held to prevent any journalist from sending special and exclusive information to any quarter.

(e) Supplying or accepting instructions to supply correspondence on terms below those recognised in his correspondence district, which terms, in case of doubt, shall be defined by the committee of the District of the Institute within which such correspondence arises, or, where there is no District, by the Council.

3   Membership or the designations of membership of the Institute may not be used for the purpose of advertising or promoting any business not directly or legitimately connected with journalism or literature. The Council shall have power to decide whether, in the circumstances of any given case, a Member has made such use of his membership as is contrary to the provisions or Article 3 of the Charter. The Council shall have power to take such steps as they may find necessary or desirable for dealing with infractions of Article 3 and S.O. 51.

Appendix 5:
International Federation of Journalists Declaration of Principles on the Conduct of Journalists

This international declaration is proclaimed as a standard of professional conduct for journalists engaged in gathering, transmitting, disseminating and commenting on news and information in describing events.

1. Respect for truth and for the right of the public to truth is the first duty of the journalist.
2. In pursuance of this duty, the journalist shall at all times defend the principles of freedom in the honest collection and publication of news, and of the right to fair comment and criticism.
3. The journalist shall report only in accordance with facts of which he/she knows the origin. The journalist shall not suppress essential information or falsify documents.
4. The journalist shall only use fair methods to obtain news, photographs and documents.
5. The journalist shall do the utmost to rectify any published information which is found to be harmfully inaccurate.
6. The journalist shall observe professional secrecy regarding the source of information obtained in confidence.
7. The journalist shall be alert to the danger of discrimination being furthered by media, and shall do the utmost to avoid facilitating such discriminations based on, among other things, race, sex, sexual orientation, language, religion, political or other opinions, and national and social origins.
8. The journalist shall regard as grave professional offenses the following: plagiarism; malicious misinterpretation; calumny; libel; slander; unfounded accusations; acceptance of a bribe in any form in consideration of either publication or suppression.

9. Journalists worthy of the name shall deem it their duty to observe faithfully the principles stated above. Within the general law of each country the journalist shall recognise in professional matters the jurisdiction of colleagues only, to the exclusion of any kind of interference by governments or others.

(Adopted by 1954 World Congress of the IFJ. Amended by the 1986 World Congress)

Appendix 6:
Law and Ethics for Periodical Journalism

LAW AND ETHICS ASSESSMENT: CORE UNITS

DEFAMATION

List the three main defences to a libel action.

1. *Justification (or truth)*;
2. *fair comment*;
3. *privilege*.

Proving truth in substance and in fact is an absolute defence. Fair comment must be on matter of public interest; based on true fact or on privileged material, must be writer's honestly held opinion, made without malice; privilege can be either absolute as in reports of judicial proceedings, or qualified.

State the requirements for a successful defence of absolute privilege in reports of judicial proceedings.

Proceedings must have been open to the public and reports must be fair, accurate and contemporaneous (i.e. in the first possible edition of the publication).

State the requirements necessary for a successful defence of unintentional defamation to a libel action.

The words complained of were published innocently and without malice and that the publisher can show we took all reasonable care; an offer of amends was made as soon as possible.

Describe the guide-lines to determine whether a statement is defamatory.

A statement is defamatory if it does one or more of the following: exposes a person to hatred, ridicule or contempt; causes him to be shunned or avoided; lowers him in the estimation of right-thinking members of society generally; disparages him in his business, trade, office or profession.

Explain what the plaintiff has to prove to be successful in a libel action.

The plaintiff has to prove that (a) the statement is defamatory; (b) that it has been reasonably understood to refer to him/her; and (c) that it has been published to a third person.

Describe the main difference between libel and slander.
Libel is a defamatory statement in permanent form, including pictures, cartoons, broadcasts, and public performances of plays. Slander is a defamatory statement that is spoken or made in some other transient form (e.g. gesture).

Explain what is meant by libel by innuendo.
Libel by an innuendo means that statements which themselves appear to be innocuous have a defamatory meaning to those with special knowledge. For example to say that a person regularly visits certain premises is, on the surface, safe but would be a libel by innuendo to those who knew the premises were used as a brothel.

Name the defence to a libel action arising out of a report of the proceedings at a general meeting of a public company.
Qualified privilege.

List the requirements for a defence to a libel action on the grounds of qualified privilege.
The reports must be fair and accurate and published without malice; publication must not have been prohibited by law and must be of public concern or publication for the public benefit. On some occasions the complainant has a right of reply.

Define the defence of consent.
Consent (volenti no fit injuria) can be a defence if the journalist can prove that the complainant agreed to publication of the actual libel and not simply to the interview.

State the length of time within which a plaintiff must normally issue a writ for libel.
One year, unless the libel is repeated in which case the time begins to run again.

List the four occasions on which slander will be actionable without proof of damage.
An imputation that the complainant has committed a crime punishable by death or imprisonment; that he/she is suffering from a contagious or objectionable disease, e.g. AIDS, venereal disease; an imputation in the case of a woman that she is adulterous or unchaste; a statement calculated to disparage a person in his/her office, profession, calling, trade or business.

List three categories of general damages as remedies in a libel action.
Contemptuous, nominal, compensatory, aggravated, exemplary.

Name the defence available to a journalist facing a libel action arising out of the review of a film, book, stage play and other works of criticism.
Fair comment.

Explain what is meant by libel by juxtaposition in copy.
Statements which in themselves are accurate can have a defamatory meaning when juxtaposed in such a way as to impute discreditable conduct e.g. a paragraph reporting that a company is in financial difficulties followed by one

saying that its former finance director has moved to live in another country, particularly one from which he is unlikely to be extradited.

Describe the circumstances in which a picture or cartoon could be held to be defamatory.

If the picture or cartoon suggests that an identifiable person and/or place in the illustration is associated with defamatory allegations in accompanying copy – a photograph of a police officer against a story about police corruption; a story about fraud illustrated by clearly identifiable premises not connected with the allegations.

State the protection given to reports of Parliamentary proceedings, except in Hansard.

Qualified privilege.

Explain what is meant by Payment into Court as a defence to a libel action.

The defendant may pay money into court at any time after he has entered an appearance to satisfy the plaintiff's claim. If the plaintiff accepts the money the proceedings end. If, at the end of the trial, the plaintiff is awarded the same or less than the money paid into court he will be entitled to the sum awarded and will have to pay the costs incurred by the defendant after the date of payment in.

Define the legal term *Without Prejudice* in libel actions.

This term is used to protect the writer of a document (e.g. a proposed apology and/or correction) against it being construed as an admission of liability.

State what you understand by the legal meaning of malice.

This means in simple terms that the journalist is offering a point of view and is not using his position as a journalist for personal advantage or out of personal spite. Proof of malice can destroy the defences of qualified privilege and fair comment.

You are sub-editing a story about alleged doping of race horses and the reporter has written: 'The jockey told me that at least two trainers at a (named) stables are thought to be involved.' Describe the steps you would take to make the copy legally safe.

You cannot get round libel laws by not naming people. If the trainers can be identified the reporter is taking a risk. The copy could be made safer by removing the name of the stables.

You are passing a page for print and read a story about a worker dying shortly after being injured at a factory. The sub-editor's headline reads: WORKER KILLED BY FAULTY MACHINERY based on an unattributed comment. Explain the changes you believe necessary to the headline to make it legally safe.

The headline could be construed as alleging negligence by the employers and/or the manufacturer and is unsafe, particularly because the comment is unattributed. The headline should be rewritten to omit any suggestion that the man's death was caused by the fault of anybody or anything until the exact cause is known. (A good sub-editor would also consider changes to the copy.)

MALICIOUS (INJURIOUS) FALSEHOODS

Name the three types of proceedings that can be taken against journalists who publish damaging, though not defamatory, statements about people.

Injurious falsehoods of Slander of title, Slander of goods and malicious falsehoods.

State what the plaintiff must prove in an action for injurious falsehood?

The publication of a false statement, either in writing or orally, to a third party; the defendant was actuated by express malice, and – subject to the Defamation Act 1952 – he has suffered monetary loss.

State what legal action faces a journalist who wrongly reports that an accountant has retired?

An action for malicious falsehood; the statement is not defamatory but it can result in monetary loss.

You are sub-editing a product review that claims that a new piece of electrical equipment is not only inferior to similar products but is dangerous and could cause injury to users. State what action you would take to make the copy legally safe.

If the statement about the product is false the manufacturer could sue for slander of goods; but the additional problem here is that the statement disparages the trader and, therefore, really amounts to a libel. Unless there was positive proof of the dangers the claim should be struck out.

State what defences are open to a journalist involved in an action for injurious falsehood.

There are no special defences, the burden of proof is on the plaintiff to prove that the statement is untrue and was published with malice.

COPYRIGHT

State the owners of the copyright in the following: (a) a reader's letter, (b) a press release about a new product, and (c) an unsolicited feature.

The Copyright, Designs and Patents Act 1988 states that the author of a work is the first owner of any copyright in it. In the case of (a) and (c) the copyright belongs to the writer; in (b) it would belong to the writer's employer – assuming the press release was written as part of the writer's employment.

Describe the difference in copyright law between 'all rights' and 'first rights'.

The assignment of 'all rights' by the author of a work gives the new copyright owner the exclusive right to publish the work anywhere in the world at any time and in any form. The holder of 'first rights' has the right to first publication of the work anywhere in the world. This should not be confused with First European Serial Rights which gives the right to first publication only in the E.C.

Name the owner of the copyright in an employee's work.

Copyright in an employee's work is owned by his/her employer.

You have attended a speech made by a man well-known to your readers and you have recorded it in your notebook. State the owner of the copyright in the speech.

The speaker owns the copyright unless he was speaking as an employee and then the copyright would belong to his employer. The reporter also would probably obtain copyright in his report (which might be regarded as a literary work). However, journalists can publish speeches for the purpose of reporting current events unless the speaker has prohibited it.

State the owner of the copyright in a photograph taken in June 1989.

Copyright belongs to the person who commissioned the photograph, subject to any agreement to the contrary or to the owner of the material upon which it was taken.

A freelance journalist telephones you with an idea for a feature. State the owner of the copyright in that idea.

There is no copyright in ideas communicated in this situation.

TRESPASS

State the civil law wrong (tort) perpetrated by a journalist who enters a person's land without permission by pretending to be a gas inspector.

He must be aware that the owner would not have let him enter if the owner had known the truth of his identity otherwise there is no need for the deceit.

Explain why the sign TRESPASSERS WILL BE PROSECUTED is a legal nonsense.

The general rule is that trespass is a civil law wrong (tort) and the owner of the premises would have to sue in the civil courts for damages and/or an injunction; prosecution is a criminal law procedure.

Explain the legal position of a journalist who enters a person's premises without permission but for the legitimate purpose of news gathering.

The law would presume a general or implied licence to enter.

ETHICS

Name the organisation that replaced the Press Council to adjudicate on complaints.

The Press Complaints Commission.

Describe your publication's policy on publishing details of a person's race and/or colour.

No outline response to this can be given to assessors but candidates must demonstrate a clear knowledge and understanding of the publication's policy, whatever it is.

Describe the action you would take when handling a news story that is critical of a product marketed by a major advertiser in your publication.

Responses as above.

List the occasions when it could be permissible to make enquiries into an individual's private life without his or her consent.

According to the Code of Practice adopted by editors such occasions could be justified in the public interest when:

1. *detecting or exposing crime or serious misdemeanour;*
2. *detecting or exposing seriously anti-social conduct;*
3. *protecting public health and safety;*
4. *preventing the public from being misled by some statement or action of the individual.*

State the action you would take when sub-editing a news story that identified a relative of a man convicted of theft but who had no actual connection with the story.

Answers might vary but the Code of Practice says that such identification should be avoided unless it is necessary for the full, fair and accurate reporting of the crime or legal proceedings.

List the questions you would ask before using a photograph of a child under the age of 16 taken in a school playground.

Children should not be approached or photographed at school without the permission of the school authorities; nor should they be photographed for stories involving the child's personal welfare in the absence of or without the consent of a parent or other responsible adult. Questioners should check that such precautions have been taken.

Describe your response to an informant who seeks assurances that you will not disclose your source of information.

Journalists have a moral obligation to protect sources of confidential information. Journalists could attempt to persuade an informant to go 'on the record' for the sake of accuracy; could also tell informant that journalist must feel free to check accuracy of information from other sources though confidentiality will be maintained.

A contact offers you confidential information concerning practising doctors who are being treated for AIDS. State your response and the action you would take.

In the High Court in November 1987 Mr Justice Rose ruled that the public interest in maintaining the confidentiality of patients' hospital records far outweighed the public interest in the freedom of the press. A health authority was entitled to an injunction preventing publication of a story identifying two practising doctors who were victims of AIDS using information obtained through a breach of confidence. The candidate's response should show knowledge and understanding of the implications of this decision.

Specify your publication's policy on correcting factual inaccuracies.

No outline response is possible, but candidates should show a knowledge and understanding of the procedure for correcting mistakes of fact.

State what action you would take when receiving a complaint from a reader that he/she had been libelled.

Practice will vary but candidates should demonstrate the need for the complaint to be made to the editor in writing; no apology or correction should be made at this stage without legal advice.

Your news editor wants a photograph of a man well-known to your readers who has died, and an interview with his wife. Describe your reactions to these instructions.

Responses will vary but journalists should show some awareness of the guidelines on unnecessary intrusion on private grief. Candidates could suggest contacting alternative sources for the photograph. The question of the interview is more difficult: some candidates might suggest that an initial attempt be made but that the matter should not be pressed if the wife was obviously unwilling to be interviewed.

LAW AND ETHICS ASSESSMENT: NEWS AND FEATURE WRITING

DEFAMATION

Your publication receives a tip-off that a senior director at a major company known to your readers has been sacked. You try to get confirmation but his office will say only that he is not available for comment. After the story is published the director's lawyer claims that the man was not sacked but his contract had expired and was not being renewed. State the reason why your original statement is defamatory.

The original statement is defamatory because it is untrue (assuming the lawyer is telling the truth) and, therefore, disparages the director in his office, profession or trade. Sacking is an emotive term suggesting wrongdoing or unfitness for office.

During a debate in the House of Commons an MP makes a scathing attack on the chief executive of a company known to your readers and calls him 'a slippery, unscrupulous little spiv'. You carry out a follow-up interview with the MP during which he repeats the allegations and says: 'It's true and you can quote me because I can prove it.' Explain the position in the law of defamation of (a) the MP and (b) the journalist in making and repeating such a comment.

The MP is protected by absolute (Parliamentary) privilege for his remark made during the debate in the House of Commons and, therefore, he could not be sued for it. However he would not be protected at all when making the same remark outside Parliament and he could be sued. The journalist would have a defence of qualified privilege for his/her report of the debate provided it complied with the requirements of that defence; but he/she would not be protected for reporting any defamatory statements made by the same MP outside the proceedings of Parliament and should be particularly careful to make it clear in any report that the comments were made by the MP in Parliament; the journalist also should be careful not to include in his/her report any defamatory comments made by the MP during the follow-up interview.

A reader writes a letter for publication in which he complains that a company, which he names, is not carrying out statutory health and safety at work regulations and that a number of employees have been injured as a result. State the action you would take in writing a report for publication bearing in mind the laws of libel and slander.

The allegations are prima facie defamatory of the company because they could injure its trading reputation, they could also be disparaging of any executive responsible for health and safety requirements. The only defence would be difficult to prove without documentary and/or firsthand witness prepared to give evidence acceptable to the court. The fact that some employees might have been injured at work does not prove it was because of the company's negligence. The journalist also should question the motives of the letter writer,

State the possible defence(s) open to a leader writer who claims that because a company employs no 'black' workers its employment policy is racist.

The possible defences would be justification or fair comment. Justification would be an absolute defence but the journalist would need positive proof of the truth of the allegation; fair comment would succeed only if the facts again were provably true. The danger is in assuming that because a company employs no black workers it has a racist employment policy.

A contact tells you in an off-the-record chat that an electrical product from one of your advertisers is known by them to be unsafe without modification but that they have decided not to withdraw it from the market for 'purely commercial reasons'. State the considerations for a journalist handling this information.

The allegations are disparaging not only of the company's product but also of its trading reputation because they impute dishonest and discreditable business conduct (i.e. they are prepared to go on marketing a product knowing it to be unsafe.) The allegations could be published only if the journalist is convinced he has a defence. The source of the information is unreliable for any defence of justification because of its 'unattributable' basis and proving truth by other means would be difficult. The journalist could have the product independently tested but that would not necessarily prove the truth of the manufacturer's dishonest motives.

Explain what defence, if any, you would have to reporting that a man who had been appointed head of a children's home had a 'spent' conviction for offences against boys.

Even though the conviction is 'spent' the journalist would have a defence of justification (truth) unless the man could prove that publication had been actuated by malice. In such a case as this it is unlikely the man would be able to prove any improper motive.

You write a story that at least one of the partners in a City company has been suspended over allegations of insider dealing. You name the company but not the partner(s). Describe the dangers in using this approach to avoid a possible libel action.

You cannot get round the libel laws by not naming people. The test is one of identification which does not have to be by name. The plaintiff has to prove only that the statement has been reasonably understood to refer to him/her. In this case it is possible that all the partners in the City company could sue.

In a personal opinion column you write: 'Of course, we all know that the vast majority of accountants are on the fiddle and are lining their pockets with money that really belongs to their clients.' Summarise the likelihood of a possible successful libel action by one or more accountants.

Although it is possible for people to be identified as members of a group or class it is most unlikely that any one or more accountants could claim that he/she had been libelled by this statement because the group/class is far too wide. The reference would have to be much more precise e.g. to a group practice or area where only a small number of accountants carried on business.

Define the proof required in publishing stories based on rumour and/or speculation.

The journalist has to prove not only that the rumour and/or speculation exists but that any defamatory content is also provably true. Lord Devlin said 'For the purpose of the law of libel a hearsay statement is the same as a direct statement, and that is all there is to it.' However, proof that the purpose of publishing the rumour was to discredit it could remove any defamatory meaning from it.

List the difficulties facing a journalist who wants to plead the defence of justification to a libel action.

Journalists wishing to plead justification (truth) as a defence to a libel action should bear in mind:

1. *the burden of proof is on him/her*
2. *the cost of preparing such a defence*
3. *the difficulty in relying on witnesses who might have moved while others might have died*
4. *believing something to be true – particularly information received in confidence – and being able to prove it to the satisfaction of a court*
5. *the unpredictability of juries and the unknown amount of damages likely to be awarded in the event of an unsuccessful defence*
6. *the risk of increased damages consequent upon insisting that the statement could be justified when clearly it could not*
7. *the fact that even if successful the journalist will still incur considerable legal costs.*

State the defence available to a journalist who publishes defamatory material with permission of the plaintiff.

Volenti non fit injuria (consent) is a defence available to a journalist who publishes defamatory statements with the plaintiff's permission provided that the statements refer only to the plaintiff; the consent applied only to the published libel and not to any additional material the journalist might wish to include. Consent should where possible be obtained in writing; simply granting an interview during which defamatory statements are made should not be regarded as consent to publish them, nor should a refusal to comment.

What defence is available to a publication that offers a 'right of reply' to a person attacked in its columns?

Qualified privilege protects bona fide replies to defamatory statements made on the principle of 'right of reply'. A person whose reputation is attacked in a publication can reply to those criticisms and the editor can plead qualified privilege in defence.

Describe the steps you would take before publishing information 'leaked' to you by the secretary of a local authority press officer.

Information issued to the press by local government executives is covered by qualified privilege provided such executives are authorised to issue information to the press. The privilege does not extend to 'leaked' information nor does it give protection to matter passed on by unauthorised people or by junior officials. In this case, therefore, the journalist would have no qualified privilege defence and would need to check the information through an approved source or to be able to defend its publication in some other legally recognised way.

Define the position of a trade union in the law of libel when it accuses a publication of printing defamatory comments about its activities.

A trade union has no corporate legal personality and cannot, therefore, bring an action for libel. However this does not stop a union official from instituting a libel action in his/her own name even though he/she has not been named but argues that he/she has been libelled by innuendo.

State what action might be taken against a journalist who is investigating demands by some employees that a worker should be suspended from duty because he is thought to be suffering from AIDS.

The worker could consider instituting proceedings for slander if the defamatory comments were published to a third person. He would not be required to prove special damage – sometimes necessary in slander actions – if AIDS is now regarded as 'a contagious disease' for the purpose of defamation proceedings.

Describe the difficulty facing a journalist who makes a defamatory comment in a personal column about someone whom he refers to simply as AB.

The question is one of identification. Would the initials reasonably lead people who knew the plaintiff to believe he/she was the person being referred to?

Name the defence available to a journalist who, in order to illustrate a point in a feature on crime in industry, creates a believably fictitious character but who is subsequently threatened with an action for libel by a person with that name who claims he has been identified as being involved in criminal behaviour.

The defence would be one of unintentional defamation. The journalist must show that the words complained of were published innocently of the plaintiff and that an offer of amends was made. This means offering to publish a suitable correction and apology and to pay legal costs. But the publisher must show that he/she took 'all reasonable care in relation to the publication' by checking that no obvious misunderstanding or confusion could exist. This could be difficult to prove.

List the people who can be sued for publication of a defamatory statement.
Everybody who has taken some part in its publication can be sued e.g. the journalist, editor, proprietor, printers and newsagents, though the latter category would have a defence of innocent dissemination in most cases. Refer also to the Defamation Act 1996.

You write a story based on information contained in a published report that is covered by qualified privilege. The editor writes a leader based on your story. Subsequently the facts on which the story and the leader were based are shown to be untrue. State the defence open to the reporter and the editor.
Provided the facts were accurately reported in the publication the reporter and the editor would have a defence of (a) qualified privilege and (b) fair comment.

Clarify the need to distinguish between fact and comment in an opinion piece.
Expressions of opinion can be defended as fair comment provided that the facts on which the opinion is based are also stated in some way and are provably true or are contained in privileged material. Comment without fact cannot be defended as fair comment, and the journalist would have to reply on justification.

State the protection given in the law of defamation to a report of a public meeting held in an English town but to which a journalist had not been invited.
A fair and accurate report of the proceedings at any public meeting held in the United Kingdom is protected by qualified privilege, provided the meeting was bona fide and lawfully held for a lawful purpose and for the furtherance or discussion of any matter of public concerns whether admission to the meeting was general or restricted.

During a crown court trial the defendant makes a defamatory attack on an MP who is in no way connected with the defendant or the trial. State the defence available to a journalist who reports the comment and is threatened with an action for libel by the MP.
Absolute privilege applies to statements made in judicial proceedings regardless of whether the statements are true or false. A journalist would, therefore, have this defence in this case, provided the report was fair and accurate, published contemporaneously and that the court was open to the public.

Explain the effect on the defences of fair comment and qualified privilege if the plaintiff can show that defamatory statements about him/her had been published with malice.

Proof that when the journalist made the statements complained of he or she was actuated by malice will destroy the defences of fair comment and qualified privilege.

Define the purpose of compensatory damages in an action for libel.

Compensatory damages are awarded as an attempt to restore the plaintiff's reputation to what it would have been had the libel not been published.

List the circumstances in a libel action where exemplary (or punitive) damages may be awarded.

Exemplary (or punitive) damages may be awarded:

1. *Where the plaintiff proves that the journalist published defamatory material because he considered the advantage of gaining, for example, increased sales outweighed the disadvantages of loss;*
2. *if compensatory damages would be insufficient to punish the journalist.*

MALICIOUS FALSEHOODS

Summarise the distinction between an action for defamation and one for malicious falsehood.

In an action for defamation the plaintiff has to prove that the words are defamatory; in malicious falsehood there is no such requirement;

In defamation the defendant has to prove the truth of the statement, but in malicious falsehood it is up to the plaintiff to prove they are false;

Malice is an essential part of a claim for malicious falsehood, but not always in defamation;

In malicious falsehood the plaintiff often has to prove he has suffered damage but in defamation does not;

An action for malicious falsehood survives after the plaintiff's death but an action for defamation does not;

Damages in malicious falsehood are restricted to pecuniary loss but in defamation they will include an amount for injury to the plaintiff's feelings.

Define the action that could be taken by a wine merchant who was criticised for selling vintage wine that was below the standard for that particular year.

If the criticism is only of the wine merchant's products he would have an action for malicious falsehood if he could prove that the statement was false and had been made maliciously with intent to injure. However, if the statement inferred that his judgement in selecting wine was so bad that it could reflect on the conduct of his business and show he was inefficient it would be a libel.

State the purpose for awarding damages in an action for malicious falsehood and how it differs from an award of damages in a libel action.

The purpose of awarding damages in an action for malicious falsehood is to make up for any actual or probable pecuniary loss; in libel the purpose is to compensate for injury to the plaintiff's personal feelings.

Describe the dangers for a journalist in comparing a product from manufacturers A with a similar product from manufacturers B.
The journalist needs to distinguish between what would be regarded generally as a 'trader's puff' i.e. a simple exaggeration of a product's worth and what would be regarded as denigration of product B. The test is whether the reasonable man would believe the claim was seriously being made. If that is the case then manufacturers A could have a claim for slander of goods. Malice could be shown if the journalist knew the statement was untrue or he had been told by manufacturers B they were alleged to be false.
State why a defence of fair comment would not apply in an action for malicious falsehood.
The defence would not apply because the basis of an action for malicious falsehood is that the facts are not true; a defence of fair comment necessarily requires that the facts on which the comment is based are true.

TRESPASS

State what action could be taken against a journalist who secretly places a microphone in a man's office.
An action for trespass and a claim for damages.
During an industrial dispute at a factory a journalist stands on public ground and uses binoculars to 'spy' into the factory compound. State what action, if any, can be taken by the factory's management.
No action can be taken against the journalist simply for 'snooping' on property from a place he is entitled to be.
Describe what legal action can be taken against a journalist who gains permission to enter a person's property and carries out, and reports on, observations he made that were outside the purpose of his intended visit.
No action can be taken in law because the reporter was not trespassing. He was not doing anything he was not invited to do and his motives for being on the property were irrelevant.

COPYRIGHT

Explain the basic purpose of the law of copyright.
The basic purpose is to protect the skill, labour, time and judgment an author puts into his/her works from unlawful copying by others when the work is published.
State the copyright in the facts of a news story.
There is no copyright in the facts of a news story; copyright comes in the skill, labour, time and judgment a reporter uses in compiling his/her story.
You write a feature as a freelance journalist and send it to a magazine and are paid £200 for it. State the owner of the copyright in that feature.

The freelance journalist owns the copyright unless there has been some assignment of it.

A magazine's editorial office can receive scores of Press Releases every day, some of which will be used and others not. State the owners of the copyright in the Press Releases that are used by the magazine.

The writers of the Press Releases will own the copyright in them unless they are working as employees in which case their employers will own the copyright. The magazine is simply being given a license to publish them on one occasion.

State the owner of the copyright in tables of product prices compiled by a magazine's editorial office.

The magazine will own the copyright in the compilation.

You spend a great deal of time and energy on writing a 3,000 word feature which, when published, you consider has been so badly sub-edited that it reflects adversely on your professional integrity. State what action you can take in the law of copyright to redress your grievance.

None. The only possible legal action in such a case as this would be to sue for breach of moral rights i.e. that the work had been subject to derogatory treatment, but moral rights do not apply to an employee's work, or to any other work made for the purpose of publication in magazines, newspapers and so on, or made available with the consent of the author for such purposes.

After an interview with a person well known to your readers you write a profile in such a way that it appears to have been written by the person himself. He claims it has misrepresented what he told you and threatens to sue. List two possible legal actions against you.

1. *He might have an action for breach of moral rights on the grounds that the work is falsely attributed to him;*
2. *he might have an action for libel if the article defames him in any way.*

A magazine for the catering industry produces a report about the eating habits of Britain's teenagers and several other publications publish stories based on the magazine article and use extracts from it. State the defence in copyright to such a practice.

There is a defence of fair dealing for the purpose of reporting current events provided the source of the information is sufficiently acknowledged and the extracts do not constitute a substantial part of the original.

Outline the defence of 'public interest' in an action for infringement of copyright.

The 1988 Copyright Act does not define the 'public interest' defence but does indicate that it can be available in some situations where the court accepts the public interest in revealing certain information can be greater than any argument of breaches of confidence and/or copyright. It will arise particularly, therefore, in attempts to stop journalists publishing sensitive information obtained by 'leaks' of confidential documents.

List the remedies that can be imposed for breaches of copyright.
The copyright owner can obtain an injunction to stop infringement of his copyright:

1. *damages for infringement and account of profits;*
2. *an order for possession of the infringing copies;*
3. *prosecution and fine and/or imprisonment.*

BREACH OF CONFIDENCE

Outline the basis of the grounds on which a plaintiff might bring an action for breach of confidence.
The basis of such a claim is a right to privacy or the protection of private 'property' in the sense that information is regarded as a kind of property.
Distinguish between information which is interesting to the public and that which is in the public interest in the law of confidence.
This is the difference between stories that appeal to the public's curiosity in other people's private lives and those that open otherwise secret issues to public debate.
State how a company can attempt to stop publication of material gained by breach of confidence.
The company can apply to the High Court for an interim injunction until the action can be tried in an attempt to make the interim injunction permanent.
List two types of legal action that can be taken to protect privacy in information.
There is no right to privacy in law but people and/or organisations can seek to protect privacy by actions for trespass, copyright, data protection.
You receive documents and letters that have been stolen from a company known to your readers. State whether you can safely publish all or any of the information contained in the stolen material.
The company could apply to the High Court for an injunction to prevent publication of such information but the granting of an injunction is not automatic. A national newspaper was able to publish letters which had been stolen from a homosexual lover.
Your publication receives information as a result of private telephone taps which includes defamatory material about a man well-known to your readers. State whether stories using such information can be safely published.
This presents a dilemma for journalists; attempts to check the accuracy of the information before publication alert the subject to the journalist's possession of it and steps can be taken to seek an injunction to stop publication. Publishing without checking could lead to an action for libel.
The accountant of a large company resigns and hands to your magazine some of the firm's documents which indicate that the company had been attempting to avoid tax. The company threatens to seek an injunction to restrain publication on

the grounds of breach of confidence. Outline your assessment of the likelihood of the application being successful.

There is no absolute certainty in the answer. In some cases the court will rule that in such a situation they have to balance the public interest in disclosure against the public interest in maintaining confidence. The test appears to be whether any misconduct ought in the public interest to be disclosed to others.

TRIBUNALS

State the protection given to reports of tribunals set up either under Act of Parliament or by other means.

Qualified privilege attaches to a fair and accurate report of the proceedings of such tribunals, but publications are required to give a 'right of reply' to defamatory allegations, if requested. However, reports should contain only those matters that are relevant to the decision and should not contain anything that is 'not of public concern and the publication of which is not for the public benefit'.

Explain the difficulties that can face a journalist reporting the proceedings of a tribunal and in which there is information given that could prejudice a trial or inquest.

The difficulty is in determining whether the tribunal is a court within the terms of the Contempt of Court Act 1981. If it is then the tribunal should issue an order under S4 of the Act postponing the reporting of the information. If it is not a court it cannot issue such an order and the journalist can report the material provided that it could not be considered prejudicial to any legal proceedings.

List two types of cases heard by industrial tribunals.

Unfair dismissal, sexual and/or racial discrimination in the workplace, matters involving redundancy/payments, problems of health and safety at work, claims for equal pay.

List the decisions that can be reached by a tribunal.

The tribunal can:

1. *reserve its decision for later publication;*
2. *announce a decision briefly and publish a fuller decision later;*
3. *announce its decision in full immediately.*

List the occasions when an industrial tribunal can sit in private.

1. *In the interests of national security;*
2. *to prevent a breach of law;*
3. *to prevent a breach of confidence;*
4. *where disclosure of information would prejudice an employer's interests.*

Name the defence available to a journalist for a report of a local inquiry set up by a Government minister.

A fair and accurate report of such an inquiry would be covered by qualified privilege for any defamatory matter in it.

LOCAL AUTHORITIES

State the occasions when the Press can be excluded from meetings of local authorities.
The Press must be excluded from meetings of county and district councils when confidential information is likely to be discussed. Additionally a local authority may pass an exclusion order when 'exempt information' is to be discussed. Such information would include those matters regarding personnel, council tenants, individual child welfare cases, investigation of offences, purchasing of goods, services and property.
State the protection given to reports of sub-committees of county and district councils.
Qualified privilege.
Define the action a journalist can take if he/she believes a local authority is not complying with the law regarding the rights of journalists.
In such a situation a journalist could apply to the Queen's Bench Division of the High Court for an order of mandamus compelling the authority to comply with its legal obligations.

COMPANY MEETINGS

Define what rights, if any, a journalist has to attend a general meeting of a company known to his/her readers.
Journalists have no rights to attend such meetings but they can be invited to do so.
Name the protection given to journalists who report the proceedings of a general meeting of a public company.
Qualified privilege, subject to 'right of reply' if requested.
Explain the action a company can take when involved in a take-over battle to inform the Press about the details involved.
The company can hold meetings with some shareholders to explain the terms of the offer only if the Press is invited, under the terms of the City Code on Take-overs and Mergers.
State the dangers in implying that a company has gone into members' voluntary liquidation and is, therefore, in financial difficulty.
This type of liquidation takes place when a company decides to cease trading for reasons other than insolvency e.g. retirement of a senior member or because of a merger. To suggest insolvency in such cases would be defamatory.

CONTEMPT AND THE LEGAL CONSEQUENCES OF NON-DISCLOSURE

State a journalist's obligation in disclosing sources of information to the police.

The journalist is under no duty to provide answers to police questions with the exception of possible breaches of Official Secrets Acts.

Outline the duty of a journalist to answer questions put by an inspector appointed by the Department of Trade and Industry to carry out investigations into alleged insider dealing.

The inspector can require anybody, including journalists, to answer the questions and produce documents. Any failure by the journalist to do this can be referred to the courts. Failure by the journalist to answer questions in court can result in punishment as though he/she had committed contempt of court. A journalist on a national newspaper was fined £20,000 in 1988 for refusing to answer questions in a similar situation.

Detail the circumstances in which a court can compel a journalist to disclose his/her sources of information.

The court can order disclosure on the following grounds:

1. *that it is necessary in the interests of justice or national security;*
2. *for the prevention of disorder or crime.*

Outline the approach taken by the courts in determining whether compelling a journalist to reveal his/her source is 'necessary in the interests of justice'.

The court will determine whether such interests in providing a name or names 'are of such prepondering importance in the individual case that the ban on disclosure imposed by the opening words of the section [10 of the Contempt of Court Act 1981] really needs to be overridden'.

State what legal action can be taken against a journalist who destroys or mutilates a document he/she has been ordered by a court to return to its owner.

In such a case the journalist would be in contempt of court.

State the action that can be taken against a journalist who destroys or mutilates a document before being ordered to return it to its owner.

The only remedy open to the owner would be a claim for damages for lost property.

State under what circumstances a journalist could be compelled, under the Police and Criminal Evidence Act 1984, to hand over special procedure material.

If the police can convince a circuit judge:

1. *there are reasonable grounds for believing a serious arrestable offence has been committed;*
2. *that the material is likely to be of substantial value to investigations;*
3. *that the material is likely to be relevant evidence;*
4. *the public interest requires an order to be made.*

Define the legal requirements under data protection legislation for journalists who store personal data on living people on computer.
Journalists using computers for such purposes need to register with the Registrar of Data Protection, as required by the Data Protection Act 1984.

OPERATION OF THE CIVIL AND CRIMINAL COURTS

State the degree of proof required in (a) civil (b) criminal trials.
(a) On a balance of probabilities; (b) beyond all reasonable doubt.
List three types of cases heard in county courts.
Contract and torts (but not libel or slander), land, trusts, mortgages, partnerships, adoption, guardianship of minors, bankruptcy, undefended divorce proceedings, some cases of racial and sexual discrimination, landlord and tenant disputes.
List two officials who deal with cases in county courts.
Registrars and judges.
State the correct form of address in copy for a county court judge.
At first mention the full name used (e.g. Judge John Jones) but later he would be referred to as Judge Jones or the judge.
List three divisions of the High Court.
The Queen's Bench, the Chancery and the Family Divisions.
List two types of cases heard in the Queen's Bench Division of the High Court.
Libel, slander, wrongful arrest, malicious prosecution, appeals on points of law from magistrates' courts and from the crown courts.
Name the court that hears appeals from the High Court in civil law matters.
The Court of Appeal, Civil Division.
Name the highest court of appeal in the UK in civil law cases.
The House of Lords, though candidates should understand that this is not all members of the House of Lords but only the Law Lords (or Lords of Appeal).
Outline the trial procedure in a magistrates' court when a defendant pleads not guilty.
The prosecution outlines the case and calls witnesses; witnesses can be cross-examined; the defence then calls its witnesses and they can be cross-examined; the prosecution has a right to make a closing speech, and the defence has the right of reply. If the defendant is found guilty the magistrates can hear a plea in mitigation; the court will also be told of any previous convictions; sentence is passed unless it is adjourned until social inquiry reports have been made. If the defendant is found not guilty he is released.
List the three types of hearings in a crown court.
Murder, manslaughter, robbery, rape and other indictable offences that must be tried at a crown court; cases sent by magistrates where there is an option; cases sent by magistrates for sentence; appeals from magistrates' courts.
List the four types of judges who preside at crown courts.

High Court, circuit, recorders and assistant recorders.

State the form of address of a High Court judge sitting in crown courts.

Mr (or Mrs) Justice followed by the surname (e.g. Mr Justice Brown, Mrs Justice Brown.

State the requirements under which juries at crown court trials are allowed to bring in majority verdicts.

The jury must have been out at least two hours and ten minutes without arrival at a unanimous verdict. The majority verdicts possible are: 11–1, 10–2; in some cases majorities of 10–1 or even 9–1 are possible but only in exceptional circumstances.

Describe the duties of (a) the judge, (b) the jury at the end of the hearing of evidence at a crown court trial.

(a) The judge sums up the case to the jury and explains points of law; (b) the jury determines guilt or innocence based on the evidence it has heard. Candidates could mention that a judge can direct a jury to bring in a not guilty verdict if he/she believes there is insufficient evidence.

Name the types of lawyers that have rights of audience at crown court trials.

Barristers only can conduct the prosecution or defence; a solicitor can appear for the defence at appeals or committals for sentence if the defendant was represented by the solicitor (or his firm) in the lower court. Candidates might show further knowledge and understanding by adding that solicitors have urged the Lord Chancellor to extend their rights to appear in higher courts.

REPORTING RIGHTS AND RESTRICTIONS

List the factors to be considered when reporting a defendant's application for bail.

Contempt of Court when reporting objections to bail because of previous convictions; also reporting anything other than 'arrangements as to bail' even when the defendant has asked for reporting restrictions to be lifted – again because of the risk of contempt.

Outline the reasons why journalists are restricted in reporting adjournments or committals for trial by magistrates to crown courts.

To avoid potential jurors at the trial being prejudiced by what they hear or read about the case before the trial opens.

List the points a journalist can report from a preliminary hearing in the magistrates' court about a case going to trial at crown court.

1. *The name of the court and names of the examining justices;*
2. *names, addresses and occupations of parties and witnesses and the ages of defendants and witnesses;*
3. *the offence or offences charged or a summary of them;*
4. *names of lawyers in the proceedings;*

5. *decision whether to commit for trial and the decisions regarding any defendants not committed;*
6. *charges on which defendant is committed, or a summary of them, and the court to which he is committed;*
7. *date and place to which any committal is adjourned*
8. *arrangements as to bail;*
9. *whether defendant was granted legal aid;*
10. *any decision about lifting reporting restrictions.*

Explain what happens at a preliminary hearing in the magistrates' court when, in a case involving two or more defendants, only one of them wants reporting restrictions lifted.

The restrictions will be lifted only if, after hearing representations from all the defendants, the magistrates believe that it is in the interests of justice that they should be.

Outline the action a journalist could consider taking if he/she believes magistrates have wrongly refused an application to lift reporting restrictions.

The journalist could seek to challenge such a refusal by applying to the Queen's Bench Division of the High Court for an order of mandamus which would make the magistrates comply with the law.

List the restrictions on reporting proceedings in youth courts.

Reports must not include the name of the juvenile, address or school; nor must reports contain any other information that would lead to the juvenile being identified. These restrictions also apply to juvenile witnesses i.e. those under eighteen years of age. Publications are not allowed to use photographs of any of the juveniles involved. It is possible for the Home Secretary or the court to lift such restrictions but only to avoid any injustice to the juvenile.

Describe the rights a journalist has in reporting details about juveniles involved as defendants or witnesses in adult courts other than an appeal from the juvenile court.

There is no automatic ban on identification but courts can order that the juvenile should not be identified.

Describe the action that can be taken by a journalist against restrictions on reporting imposed by judges in crown courts.

Journalists have a right of appeal to the Court of Appeal against a judge's decision to grant or refuse applications either to exclude the Press and public from the proceedings or to restrict reporting of a trial on indictment. There is also a right of appeal against orders made by crown court judges to impose restrictions under S4 & 11 of the Contempt of Court Act 1981, or to restrict the public to the whole or any part of the proceedings, or to restrict the reporting of any proceedings involving orders under S39 of the Children and Young Persons Act 1933.

Explain what is meant by 'the strict liability rule' in the Contempt of Court Act 1981.

It is the rule of law which treats publication of some information as contempt of court regardless of intent to interfere with the course of justice.
State the time at which liability for contempt purposes is active in civil proceedings.
Proceedings are deemed to be active for contempt purposes where the case is set down for trial, or when a date is fixed for the case to be heard.
State the time when liability for contempt ceases in civil law proceedings.
Liability ceases when the case is disposed of or proceedings are discontinued or withdrawn.
List the stages at which liability for contempt starts in criminal proceedings.
Proceedings are active when:

1. *an arrest has been made without warrant;*
2. *a warrant has been issued for arrest;*
3. *a summons has been issued or an indictment served;*
4. *an oral charge has been made.*

List the stages at which the contempt risk in criminal proceedings ends.

1. *The arrested person is released without charge;*
2. *no arrest is made within 12 months of issue of the warrant;*
3. *the case is discontinued;*
4. *the defendant is acquitted or sentenced;*
5. *he is found unfit to be tried, or unfit to plead, or the court orders the charge to lie on file.*

Define the defence of innocent publication under the Contempt of Court Act.
There is no contempt if, having taken all reasonable care, the journalist did not know and had no reason to suspect that proceedings were active. However, the burden of proof in establishing that all reasonable care was taken is on the journalist accused of contempt.
State the defence open to a journalist under contempt rules when reporting court proceedings.
The journalist is not guilty of contempt of court under the strict liability rule in respect of a fair and accurate report of legal proceedings held in public published contemporaneously and in good faith.
Outline the defence under S5 of the Contempt of Court Act 1981 for publishing information that has a bearing on legal proceedings.
The Act says that a publication made as, or as part of, a discussion in good faith of public affairs is not to be treated as contempt of court under the strict liability rule if the risk of impediment or prejudice to particular legal proceedings is merely incidental to the discussion.
Explain the protection provided to a journalist against an order of the court requiring him/her to reveal sources of information.
The Contempt of Court Act 1981 provides that no court may require a person to disclose, nor is any person guilty of contempt of court for refusing to

disclose, the source of information contained in a publication for which he is responsible, unless it is established to the satisfaction of the court that disclosure is necessary in the interests of justice or national security, or for the prevention of disorder or crime.

State the power of the courts to suppress the publication of names of people involved in legal proceedings.

S11 of the Contempt of Court Act 1981 gives power to the courts to withhold names from being mentioned in public in proceedings and to instruct journalists not to publish the names.

ETHICS

State what action you would take when offered information in return for payment about alleged corruption by some officials of a trade association in your sector.

The Press Complaints Commission states that payment for stories should not be made in such circumstances except where the material concerned ought to be published in the public interest and the payment is necessary for this to be done.

You hear rumours that a leading figure in the sector covered by your magazine is homosexual and has been seen visiting clubs and bars frequented by members of the 'gay' community. Outline your preferred response to an instruction from your editor to write an exposé about the man.

Reactions will vary: it is believed that making enquiries about the personal lives of individuals without their consent, or publishing material about them without their consent is not generally acceptable. The only basis for such enquiries would be criminal or anti-social conduct. The test here is whether the man's sexual orientation is 'anti-social' and whether it has any bearing on his ability to conduct his trade or business. There is also the question of discrimination against a person on the grounds of sexual orientation.

A reporter on a magazine read by hospital workers employed by the NHS is told to apply for a job as a voluntary ward orderly to investigate allegations that some nursing staff at a hospital for the mentally ill are using violence to control patients. Explain your response to this use of subterfuge to obtain information.

Journalists making enquiries at hospitals or similar institutions should identify themselves to a responsible official and obtain permission before entering non-public areas. There might be a case for subterfuge if routine enquiries fail to reveal evidence of alleged ill-treatment of patients and it is considered necessary in the public interest that the allegations be investigated by 'misrepresentation'.

State the guideline regarding discrimination in the Code of Practice for journalists underpinning the Press Complaints Commission.

The Press should avoid prejudicial or pejorative reference to a person's race, colour, religion, sex or sexual orientation or to any physical or mental illness or handicap.

It should avoid publishing details of a person's race, colour, religion, sex or sexual orientation, unless these are directly relevant to the story.

A reporter works on a magazine read by people involved in the financial sector and regularly receives information in advance of its general publication. Define the ethical position for that reporter in using such information for personal gain.

1. *Even where the law does not prohibit it, journalists should not use for their own profit financial information they receive in advance of its general publication, nor should they pass such information to others.*
2. *They should disclose a personal interest in shares and securities to their editors.*
3. *They should not buy or sell shares or securities about which they have recently written or about which they intend to write in the near future.*

Define your magazine's policy on a 'Right of Reply' for individuals who are personally attacked in its columns.

The Code of Practice states: A fair opportunity for reply to inaccuracies should be given to individuals or organisations when reasonably called for.

An advertiser offers to pay for a holiday for you in any country of your choice in return for favourable coverage of his products. Define your response to approaches of this kind.

Journalists should not accept favours in return for promises of coverage of an advertiser's products. Products should be discussed on their merits or otherwise. Any attempts by advertisers to obtain favourable coverage by 'bribes' and offers of favours should be reported to the editor.

A reader offers you money not to publish information which, although accurate, is discreditable of him. State your response.

Journalists should not accept gifts of any kind in return for promising either to publish or not to publish information. Such information should be considered on its merits and attempts to influence journalists by offers should be reported to the editor.

LAW AND ETHICS ASSESSMENT: SUBBING

LIBEL

Your City correspondent who is a freelance contributor writes about the surprise resignation of the chief executive of a stockbroking firm and says: For this chief executive truth was a moving target. State whether you consider such a statement is libellous and, if so, how its publication could be defended.

Certainly the statement is libellous because it would disparage the chief executive in his office, profession or trade, but whether it is legally defensible depends on the accuracy of the information on which the comment is based. *If the facts were inaccurately stated, or not referred to in the piece, then it would have to be defended on the basis of justification – and that could be immensely difficult.*

You are sub-editing a story about a fire at a factory in which a man died and the copy includes the following quote from a trade-union official: 'I knew this would happen one day. I've complained about lack of proper fire precautions here for months but the boss has turned a blind eye.' Describe the steps you would take to make this copy legally safe.

The quote as it stands is defamatory of the 'boss' because it accuses him of gross negligence. Even with a comment from him it would be unwise to publish without firm evidence of its reliability.

You are handling the layout of a centre spread on fare dodging on British Rail and you want to illustrate it with photographs of commuters who have been 'caught'. Describe the action you would take to make this legally safe.

To do this safely would involve hiring models to pose as commuters and you would need their consent in writing to having their photographs used for such a purpose. Any attempt to use photographs taken from the library should be strongly resisted.

State what defence, if any, is given to the publication of readers' letters that contain defamatory allegations.

None. The fact that the allegations are contained in a letter and not in a story or feature is irrelevant. If they are published in a magazine the victim of the libel can sue.

The headline on a news story that fraud squad officers are inquiring into the affairs of a named firm and its subsidiary companies reads: INQUIRY ON FIRM BY FRAUD SQUAD. The investigation was requested after criticisms of the chairman's statement and the accounts by a shareholder at the recent company meeting. State whether you consider that the headline is legally safe and give your reasons.

The problem here is whether a statement that the fraud squad was investigating a company's affairs meant that fraud had been committed, or whether it had been only suspected – and that would be left to the jury.

In a feature on June brides the writer interviews newly-weds Mr and Mrs John Brown and tells your readers: They have decided to rent a house called Flotsam in the picturesque village of Littlehaven for the first years. John's wife Jane said: 'The house is very nice now but when we first got it it was terrible. We've had to spend a lot of time cleaning it out and decorating it ...' Explain whether you could safely publish this comment.

It could be argued that the comment is libellous because it reflects on the dignity and cleanliness of the previous owners who, although not named, could argue that they had reasonably been identified because the house has been named. It would be safer to sub-edit the quote to leave out any misunderstanding.

You are handling the sub-editing and layout of a news page and have two stories about pubs: the first story – with an accompanying picture – announces the winner of a Pub of the Year Award and the second is a court story about a publican being convicted of selling drink to underage youths. Explain the danger in running both stories side by side.

There is the possibility of a claim for libel by juxtaposition; that the pub in the picture could be mistakenly identified as that run by the publican who had been in court. The stories should, therefore, be distinctly separated.

List suitable shorter alternatives for the following words when used in headlines:

redundant	resigns
house	light-hearted

Assessors should use discretion but should not accept sacked, home, quits, gay – because of the possible defamatory inferences.

A profile contains the expression: His name is not John Brown but it is not George Washington either. State why it would be legally unsafe to publish it.

There is a clear inference of dishonesty here and the man could sue for libel. George Washington was, of course, a man said never to have told a lie.

You are sub-editor on a Good Food Guide in which a popular writer is strongly critical of some poultry producers and says he would never eat poultry or eggs from one producer in the West Country, whom he does not name, because of 'the appalling conditions in which the livestock are kept and slaughtered'. State the legal pitfalls in publishing such a comment.

The comment is clearly defamatory and the question would rest on whether the actual West Country producer could be identified. Another question would be that of a group/class libel: in the event of there being only a small number of producers in that part of the country they might all sue. A good sub-editor would not allow such potentially damaging statements to go unchecked.

An article in a lifestyle magazine gives advice about buying homes in France, and warns readers to deal only though accredited estate agencies and adds 'There are far too many cowboys around and buyers could find themselves out of luck, out of pocket and out of home if they choose the wrong agent.' Accompanying the feature from a freelance journalist are photographs showing a number of homes in France and giving details of UK agents handling the sales. State the legal pitfalls involved in the presentation of this feature.

The danger is that the homes and agents identified by the photographs could be mistakenly associated with the 'cowboy' agents referred to in the piece and therefore it could be defamatory. Care should be taken to avoid such a danger by skilful sub-editing and layout.

As a spoof item on your gossip page you publish a story about a company called Dead-beats and claim a remarkable resemblance between its chairman, whom you call Farley Dryweather, and TV con-man Arthur Daley of the *Minder* series. You publish two photographs – one of actor George Cole (captioned Arthur Daley) and the other of a man taken from a library picture and captioned Farley Dryweather. The man in the second picture and a Mr Farley Dryweather both threaten to sue the magazine for libel. As the sub-editor handling this item state what your defence would be.

The only possible defence would be unintentional defamation of the real Mr Farley Dryweather but it is unlikely to be successful unless you could show that you did not know it was defamatory of him and that you had checked that no other Mr Farley Dryweather existed. In the circumstances it would be very difficult. A correction and apology (offer of amends) would be the most helpful defence. The man in the photograph taken from the library also could sue on the grounds that he had been identified as a 'con-man'.

MALICIOUS FALSEHOODS

You sub-edit a story from a contributor that claims a company has ceased trading. In fact, the report is inaccurate and although the founder-director has retired the company is still carrying on business. State your legal liability.

The company would have an action for malicious falsehood but would have to prove that the statement was untrue (which should not be difficult) and was published with malice.

A reporter writes that a bakery has applied for planning permission to turn its premises into a restaurant. The headline reads: Baking days are over at Browns. State the legal action the company would have against the magazine.

An action for malicious falsehood. Although the statement is inaccurate it is not defamatory and, therefore, no action for libel could be brought. The plaintiff would have to prove that the statement was untrue, that it had been made with malice (carelessly) and that it had caused financial loss.

COPYRIGHT

State the owner of the copyright in photographs commissioned from a free-lance photographer.

The photographer owns it unless he/she has agreed to assign the rights in some way.

Outline the action that should be taken by sub-editors who are responsible for commissioning photographs from commercial photographers.

Commissions should be made in writing and should spell out the ownership of copyright or any assignment of it. The letter should also include the name of the publication, the fee to be paid and details of the work required to be done.

State the owner of the copyright in photographs commissioned before 1 August 1989.

Under earlier copyright law the commissioning of photographs from commercial photographers automatically acquired the copyright, unless there was agreement to the contrary.

You sub-edit a 3,000-word feature written by a staff journalist and after it is published he complains about your handling of it and says his moral rights have been infringed. State his position, and yours, in the law of copyright.

The Copyright Act 1988 gives authors the right not to have work subjected to derogatory treatment. But moral rights do not apply to an employee's work or to work written for the purpose of publication in magazines, newspapers and so on. You are not legally obliged to defend your actions and your professional approach in such a situation is your concern.

State the owner of the copyright in a feature submitted unsolicited by a free-lance writer.

The journalist owns the copyright. The fact that it is submitted for publication indicates a licence to publish on one occasion only but it does not confer rights on the publisher.

A public relations company sends you photographs with a Press Release about a new product. Define who owns the copyright in the photographs and the Press Release.

The public relations company would own the copyright in the Press Release; ownership of the copyright in the photographs would depend on whether the PR company had acquired all rights in them. If it had not, ownership would be retained by the commercial photographer.

A staff writer prepares a profile about a person well-known to your readers and you decide to present it in such a way that it appears to have been written by the subject of the piece. He subsequently claims that his personal integrity has been damaged. State the action he could take against your magazine.

The man could claim that authorship of the article could have been falsely attributed to him.

A staff writer reviews a book and quotes short extracts from it to illustrate some of his comments. Define the defence available for publication of such extracts.

It would be regarded as fair dealing for the purpose of criticism or review and provided the extracts did not form a substantial part of the original, they could be used without the copyright owner's permission.

REPORTING RESTRICTIONS IN CIVIL AND CRIMINAL COURTS

State what action you would take when sub-editing a court story that gives reasons why the prosecution opposed bail to a defendant accused of robbery. Reporting restrictions were lifted.

The test is whether the reasons would be prejudicial to the defendant's right to a fair trial. Even where reporting restrictions have been lifted it is always considered wiser not to report reasons for the opposition to bail and such remarks should be struck out of the copy.

A youth court report does not name the offender but describes him as 'the 15-year-old son of a village headmaster'. The village is named in the report. Define the position in law of youth court reports and state what action you would take, if any, when handling this report.

Restrictions on reporting youth courts ban the use of the names, addresses and schools of any juveniles involved; they also prohibit the publication of any information that is likely to lead to their identification. In this case although reporting his age would be allowed, any mention of his relationship with a village headmaster would be unwise for fear that he could be identified from that.

A defendant is accused at crown court of four offences of theft. He pleads guilty to two of them, but not guilty to the remaining two and there has to be a trial by judge and jury. The trial is likely to go beyond your publication day and the editor wants to run the opening of it in the next edition to beat your opposition. State the necessary action to make the copy legally safe.

At this stage of the trial the jury will be unaware that the defendant has pleaded guilty to two offences of theft and reporting of that fact before the trial is over would be prejudicial and contempt of court. The reference to the guilty pleas should be struck out.

You are sub-editing a report from a freelance journalist about the divorce of a man well-known to your readers. The divorce proceedings were contested and the report gives evidence of adultery and other misconduct. State how much of the report can be safely published.

Reports of proceedings for divorce are restricted to names, addresses and occupations of parties and witnesses:

1. *a concise statement of the charges, defence and counter-charges in support of which evidence is given;*
2. *submissions on points of law and court's rulings;*
3. *the judgment of the court and the judge's observations.*

During a High Court action for negligence against his employer a man makes defamatory attacks on the managing director's wife who is in no way connected with the proceedings. State the restrictions, if any, on reporting such attacks.

There are no restrictions on reporting defamatory attacks on 'innocent third parties' who are not part of the proceedings and such attacks can be reported. The test is whether ethical considerations would guide against it.

State the considerations to be taken into account when deciding whether or not to publish a sketch of the inside of a court-room during a trial, a report of which you are to publish.

It is an offence under the Criminal Justice Act 1925 to make such a sketch with a view to publication, though use of such sketches is wide and prosecution unlikely.

TRIBUNALS

You are handling a report of an industrial tribunal at which a man is alleging unfair dismissal. His claim to being 'sacked' is contested by the employer and tribunal hearing has been adjourned. Your headline reads: MAN SACKED BY ANGRY BOSS. State the danger in writing such a headline.

The tribunal is not concluded but has simply been adjourned. The dismissal is being contested and until the tribunal announces its decision it is unwise to say the man was 'sacked'.

A freelance contributor sends you a report of the hearing of a tribunal not recognised as a court in which is included information relating to a forthcoming criminal prosecution against a man. State whether it would be legally safe to include the prejudicial material in the published report.

Tribunals that are recognised as 'courts' have the authority to issue an order under Section 4 of the Contempt of Court Act 1981 postponing reporting of information regarded as prejudicial. Tribunals that are not recognised as 'courts' do not have that power, but journalists face prosecution for contempt if such prejudicial material is published.

State the protection given to fair and accurate reports of the proceedings of tribunals set up by an Act of Parliament or by other means.

Reports are protected from actions for libel by qualified privilege.

You are handling the report of a debate at a local authority meeting and a councillor is quoted supporting the granting of planning permission for a building project. You know that the councillor is a director of the building firm concerned. State what checks you would make before deciding whether to publish the report in full.

It is a criminal offence for councillors with a pecuniary interest in any matter being discussed to take part in such a discussion or to vote, and they should declare their interest. In this case the sub-editor should:

1. *check with the reporter that the name of the councillor and the quote is accurately reported;*
2. *if it is, the matter should not be published and the editor should be informed so that he can decide what action, if any, to take.*

State whether reports of the annual general meetings of private companies can be safely published.

No. Qualified privilege protects reports of such meetings of public companies but not private ones. However, if the report contained defamatory material and a defence of qualified privilege did fail the journalist could plead a defence of justification or fair comment.

CONTEMPT OF COURT

The Court of Appeal is due to hear a civil case about the behaviour of demonstrators at a defence establishment which is of interest to your readers. Your feature writer prepares a background piece to the case in which he includes evidence ruled inadmissible in the lower court. State whether such evidence can be safely left in the copy.

You should never publish evidence that has been ruled inadmissible by a court. One possible advantage in this case is that there is no jury involved and judges might be persuaded that they are not influenced by what they read.

Your magazine receives a feature about 'lager louts' and soccer hooligans and there is a photograph of a youth called Tommy 'The Bruiser' Thomson; the caption describes him as 'turning to hooliganism after an unsuccessful career as mugger, pimp and petty thief' based on his previous convictions. Some weeks ago you carried a short paragraph reporting that he had been remanded on bail by magistrates accused of assault and attempted theft. State what action you would take when handling this feature.

The feature should not be published in its present form because it is clearly a contempt of court to refer to a defendant's previous convictions before a trial.

The police issue an appeal to readers of your magazine to be on the look-out for a gang of robbers who might try to 'fence' stolen property through your readers' retail outlets. Clarify the position in the law of contempt for publishing such appeals.

The contempt risk is not active because nobody has been arrested and the police cannot get warrants for unnamed people. Even if the contempt risk was active, the then Attorney General said when the Contempt of Court Bill was passing through Parliament that the Press would not be in danger of contempt proceedings provided they acted reasonably.

You are handling a story about one of your readers who has appeared in court accused of fraud. You know that the man has previous convictions and your headline reads: SMITH IN COURT AGAIN. State why you are in danger of proceedings for contempt of court by such a headline.

The headline is prejudicial to Smith's forthcoming trial because it points out that he has previous convictions. The word 'again' should not have been used.

ETHICS

Express the guide-line issued in the Code of Practice by the Press Complaints Commission on references to a person's race, colour, religion, sex or sexual orientation in copy.

The guide-lines state that journalists should avoid such prejudicial or pejorative references unless they are directly relevant to the story.

You report that an employer's association in your sector has appointed its first black chief executive. Justify your use of his colour in this context.

Responses will vary but assessors should be convinced that the sub-editor has a reasonable answer.

The advertising manager on your magazine attempts to put pressure on you not to publish a story that is critical of one of your major advertisers because of the damage it would do commercially. Outline your likely response to such pressure.

Responses will vary but assessors should note whether the candidate has a reasonably acceptable attitude in line with his/her publication's policy.

An advertising representative on your magazine tells you that he has sold space in the next edition provided the client's new product is given preferential treatment in the editorial columns. List reasons why you would/would not respond to this pressure.

One of the reasons for responding favourably would be that it generates goodwill and revenue; responses against would include the loss of credibility (particularly if the product is inferior), the overriding interest in news values; the need for advertising and editorial not only to appear to be independent but to be seen to be independent. Assessors should evaluate other responses according to their reasonableness.

RSA Ref. L278 (1992)

Appendix 7:
Questionnaire for refresher courses

HOW MUCH DO YOU ALREADY KNOW?

Just to get you thinking you are asked to read the following statements and then draw circles around the answers you think are the correct ones. This is not a test and no record will be made of your responses.

1 To libel people you must name them. TRUE/FALSE

2 The plaintiff has to prove a journalist intended to libel him/her. TRUE/FALSE

3 You cannot libel a company. TRUE/FALSE

4 A group of people cannot be libelled, only individuals. TRUE/FALSE

5 A journalist cannot be sued simply for repeating another person's defamatory statement. TRUE/FALSE

6 It is possible to libel a person by use of a photograph. TRUE/FALSE

7 It is libellous to write that an architect knows nothing about design. TRUE/FALSE

8 To claim that a person has Aids is not libellous if it is true. TRUE/FALSE

9 A journalist can defend a libel action by trying to prove he/she did not know a statement was libellous. TRUE/FALSE

10 It is legally safe to compare a fictitious character with a living person in an interview. TRUE/FALSE

11 A person must prove financial loss before he/she can succeed with a libel action. TRUE/FALSE

12 A critic can write what he/she likes about an actress
   provided it is 'fair'.   TRUE/FALSE

13 To write that a man was a thief if he had recently
   been convicted of theft is not libellous.   TRUE/FALSE

14 'Scandalous' is a safe way of describing business
   methods that are unethical but not illegal.   TRUE/FALSE

15 To quote a defamatory statement made by an MP in a
   Parliamentary debate is always legally safe.   TRUE/FALSE

16 A cartoon can never be the subject of a libel action. TRUE/FALSE

17 It is libellous to wrongly publish a person's death.   TRUE/FALSE

18 You cannot be sued for publishing a defamatory
   statement in an interviewee's quote if you also publish
   a denial of it by the person named in the same piece. TRUE/FALSE

19 It would be perfectly safe to describe a rising young
   pop singer as 'a 19-year-old bachelor boy who enjoys
   the gay social life of pubs and clubs'.   TRUE/FALSE

20 Readers' letters can never be the subject of a libel
   action because they are not the publication's own
   opinions or claims.   TRUE/FALSE

Appendix 8:
Sample questions on libel and other legal issues

The following situations are based on actual cases. Study each one and decide (a) whether it is defamatory or otherwise legally dangerous and (b) if you think it is, how you would handle it before it was published or how you would attempt to defend it if it had already been published. Discuss your responses with one or more other course delegates and make notes for discussion.

1 You work on a publication read by workers in the medical and health care professions and you run a story based on research claiming that red wine causes migraine and other illnesses. Your art editor (or chief sub-editor) illustrates the piece with a picture showing the label of a well-known brand of claret. The wine shippers complain.

2 You publish a report of the proceedings at a general meeting of a public company whose activities are of interest to your readers. During the meeting the chairman made a startling attack on his predecessor who had been removed in a boardroom upheaval. The current chairman claimed that the previous chairman had been found out as a 'liar and cheat' whose only interest had been in 'lining his own pockets'. Now the previous chairman has written to you demanding that you apologise for publishing the report, acknowledge that the criticisms were untrue and pay £1,000 to his favourite charity.

3 You edit an up-market glossy magazine that carries many features of interest to those readers who have a high-cost life style, including a regular restaurant review column written by a freelance noted for her aggressive style. The current issue carries a review by her that describes the food in a named restaurant as 'cooked by an incompetent chef who must have poured more brandy into himself than into the pudding', and 'unfit for consumption by anybody outside the farmyard'. The chef and the restaurateurs issue a writ for libel.

4   A freelance contributor sends you a story about the death of a man well-known to your readers. You publish it and receive a complaint from the man who tells you that he is not dead. Checks with the freelance reveal it was his mistake. The 'dead' man threatens to sue.

5   During a debate in the House of Commons on an issue in which your readers would be interested, an MP makes defamatory remarks about a leading businessman in your sector. In a follow-up interview with your reporter the MP repeats the remarks and says: 'You can quote me on that word-for-word. I stick by everything I said.' You report the MP's speech in the House and his comments later.

Appendix 9:
Sample questions on copyright

1 A girl whose wedding picture appeared in a magazine in September 1989 has just been killed in a plane crash. The picture had been taken by a freelance commercial photographer and commissioned by the girl's father. How safe (legally) would it be to publish it again with the story of her death?

2 *Office Worker News*, a weekly magazine, has carried out a survey into the attitudes of secretaries to their bosses and the way they are treated, and part of it took place in your area with some very newsworthy findings. How safe would it be to report such findings in your magazine?

3 You receive an unsolicited feature with pictures which you decide to publish. On the same day another magazine runs exactly the same piece and uses exactly the same pictures. Can you sue for breach of copyright?

4 A reporter attends a meeting of a local pressure group, at the end of which the main speaker asserts: 'If there are any reporters in the audience I must point out that nothing of what I said tonight is to be published in any way'. His speech contained some startling facts not previously made public. What action can the reporter take?

5 A reader who is not a journalist sends you a copy of a research paper he has delivered at a conference in America and it does contain some material you would like to use. However, he says in an accompanying letter that no changes can be made to the report; it has to be published as written and not amended in any way. What is your position in the law of copyright?

6 On your features page you review a book with several quotes from it. The publishers subsequently complain that your extracts are too long and out of all proportion to the length of the review itself. What is your defence to that?

7   A public relations agency sends you a copy of a brochure they have produced for a client with a handout and pictures from it. The material is of interest to you, not least because the agency's client is an advertiser in your magazine. You publish a story based on the information in the brochure and also one of the pictures. Subsequently you get a bill from the photographer, who claims you had no right to publish his picture but he will not sue if you settle his account quickly and without any argument. What do you do?

Appendix 10:
Sample questions on contempt of court

1 A magazine runs a feature on football hooliganism on the same day that a number of youths appear in crown court accused of offences arising out of events at a recent match. One of the defendants was previously interviewed by a reporter and is quoted in the feature. His lawyer tells the judge your report is a contempt of court. What might your answer be?

2 A reporter obtains confidential information that a hospital surgeon has been diagnosed as having the HIV virus but is being allowed to carry out some 'routine safe operations'. After contacting the health authority for comment and for the doctor's name he is told that an injunction will be sought to stop publication of information obtained through a breach of confidence and the judge asked to compel your reporter to reveal his source. What is your legal position?

3 Police inform you that they have acquired a warrant for the arrest of a man wanted in connection with a murder enquiry. They say he is believed to be armed and dangerous if approached. You publish that news story, naming the man, and then are told that between the time the information was given to your reporter and it being used in your latest edition the man had been arrested, charged and was to appear in court the next morning. Does this mean you are in danger of proceedings for contempt of court?

4 You are subbing a story referring to a reader who has been remanded on bail accused of theft. You know that he has several previous convictions and believe that adds weight to his present alleged offence. Your headline reads: JONES IN COURT AGAIN. Could you be accused of contempt of court?

5 A news agency sends you a court report about the trial in Birmingham of three London men accused of robbery there. The trial has been running two days when you receive an order from the crown court judge to appear before him to explain why your magazine carried a report of part of the

proceedings kept from the jury. Are you in danger of proceedings against you for contempt of court?

6   You are handed a copy of a 'leaked' document from the local regional health authority alleging large-scale theft of stores from its hospitals and you begin enquiries into the claims. Meanwhile, the authority persuades a judge to compel you to hand over the document to the court, which you do, but not before erasing a code number that would have identified your contact. Is your action a contempt of court?

Bibliography and further reading

BOOKS

Berkeley, A. (1993) *The Focal Guide to Photography and the Law*, Oxford: Focal Press.
Carter-Ruck, P.F., Walker, R. and Starte, H.N.A. (1992) *Carter-Ruck on Libel and Slander*, London: Butterworths.
Courtney, C., Newell, D. and Rasaiah, S. (1995) *The Law of Journalism*, London: Butterworths.
Crone, T. (1995) *Law and the Media*, Oxford: Focal Press.
Flint, M. (1997) *The User's Guide to Copyright*, 4th edn, London: Butterworths.
Neill, Sir B. and Rampton, R. (1983) *Duncan & Neill on Defamation*, London: Butterworths.
Robertson, G. and Nicol, A. (1992) *Media Law*, Harmondsworth, Middx: Penguin Books.
Welsh, T. and Greenwood, W. (1997) *McNae's Essential Law for Journalists*, London: Butterworths.

REPORTS

Calcutt, Sir David (1990) *Report of the Committee on Privacy and Related Matters*, Cmnd 1102, London: HMSO.
Calcutt, Sir David (1993) *Review of Press Self-regulation*, Cmnd 2135, London: HMSO.
Department of National Heritage (1995) *Privacy and Media Intrusion: The Government's Response*, London: HMSO.
Law Commission (1981) *Breach of Confidence Law*, Cmnd 8388, London: HMSO.
Lord Chancellor's Department, The Scottish Office (1993) *Infringement of Privacy*, London: COI.
National Heritage Select Committee (1993) *Privacy and Media Intrusion*, London: HMSO.

OTHER PUBLICATIONS

Howard, Clive (1994) *Journalists & Copyright*, London: National Union of Journalists.
Media Lawyer, bi-monthly newsletter for media lawyers, journalists and trainers; available from 3 Broom House, Broughton-in-Furness, Cumbria LA20 6JG.

Periodicals Training Council (1997) *Starter's Guide to NVQs in Magazines*, London: PTC.

Scottish Widows' Fund and Life Assurance Society and *Money Marketing* (1995) *A Guide to the Art of Financial Journalism*, London: Money Marketing.

Index